ideals® COUNTRY

More Than 50 Years of Celebrating Life's Most Treasured Moments

Vol. 56, No. 3

"There's a time in each year that we always hold dear—
Good old summertime."—Author Unknown

IDEALS—Vol. 56, No. 3 May MCMXCIX IDEALS (ISSN 0019-137X) is published six
times a year: January, March, May, July, September, and November by
IDEALS PUBLICATIONS INCORPORATED,
535 Metroplex Drive, Suite 250, Nashville, TN 37211.
Periodical postage paid at Nashville, Tennessee, and additional mailing offices.
Copyright © MCMXCIX by IDEALS PUBLICATIONS INCORPORATED.
POSTMASTER: Send address changes to Ideals, PO Box 305300,
Nashville, TN 37230. All rights reserved.

Title IDEALS registered U.S. Patent Office.
SINGLE ISSUE—U.S. $5.95 USD; Higher in Canada
ONE-YEAR SUBSCRIPTION—U.S. $19.95 USD; Canada $36.00 CDN (incl. GST and shipping); Foreign $25.95 USD
TWO-YEAR SUBSCRIPTION—U.S. $35.95 USD; Canada $66.50 CDN (incl. GST and shipping); Foreign $47.95 USD

Subscribers may call customer service at 1-800-558-4343 to make address changes.
Unsolicited manuscripts will not be returned without a self-addressed, stamped envelope.

ISBN 0-8249-1155-5   GST 131903775

Cover Photo
Black-Eyed Susans
Photo by Hersel Abernathy/
H. Armstrong Roberts

Inside Front Cover
MID-MORNING, DONNINGTON,
GLOUCESTERSHIRE
Charles Neal, artist
Superstock

Inside Back Cover
SUNFLOWERS
Martha Walter, artist
David David Gallery
Philadelphia/Superstock

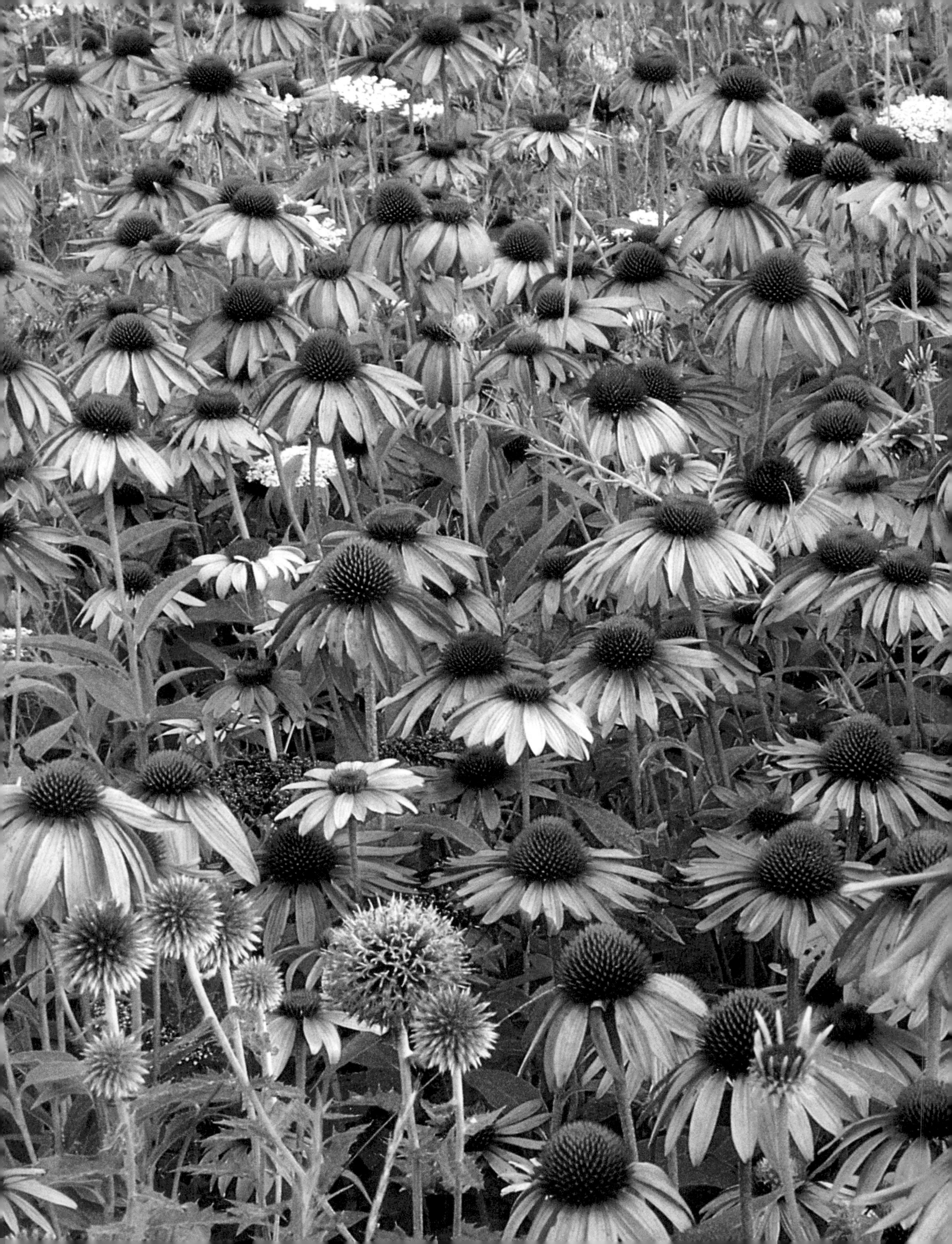

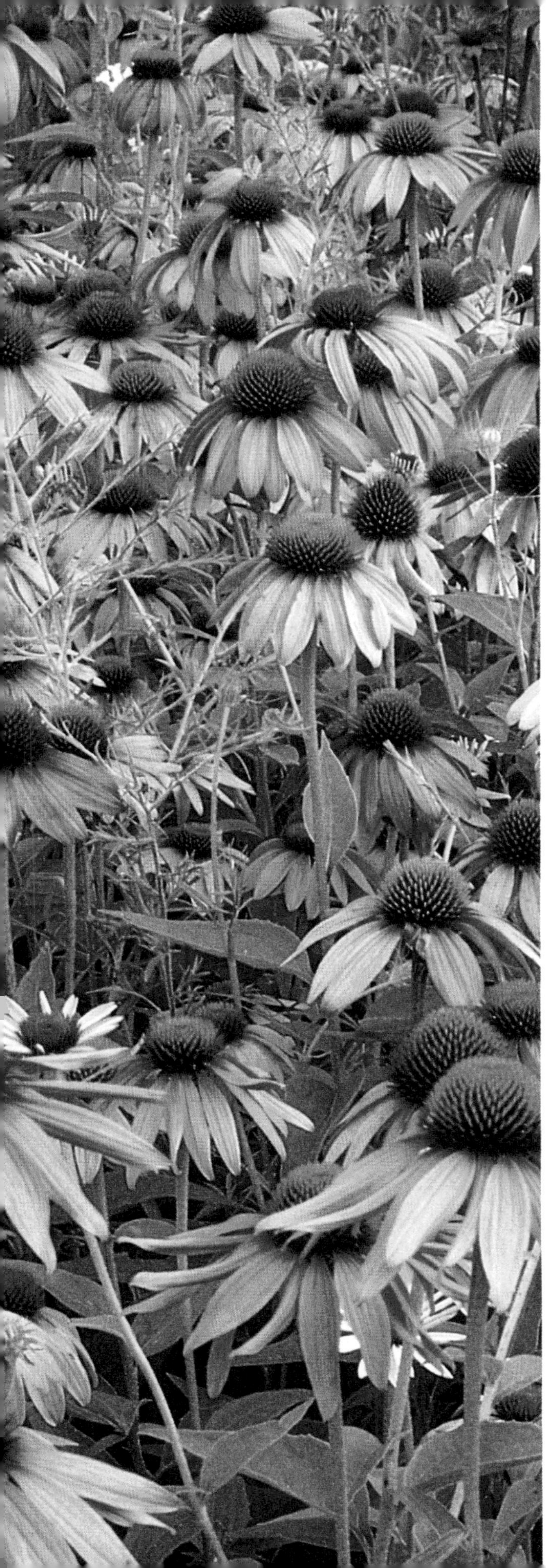

Summer Walks Again

Della Crowder Miller

Oh, Summer walks the fields again,
Companioning with sun and rain.
She scatters blossoms on the sod
To offer incense up to God.

She rides the crooning zephyr's crest
That gently rocks the robin's nest
And leaves a blush on peach and pear,
On plum and apple everywhere.

With her warm blood she tints the wing
Of redbirds and sets the lark to sing
As day appears in rose and blues
And sinks to rest in deeper hues.

She pencils dancing silhouettes
In mauve and moonlit tree-vignettes
That shimmer over shadowed pools
Where fireflies gleam in evening cools,

And where the katydids and crickets
Are trilling, clicking in the thickets.
Oh, every voice in grass and sky
Sings Summer's praise as she walks by.

A field of coneflowers in Colorado welcomes the summer.
Photo by Jessie Walker.

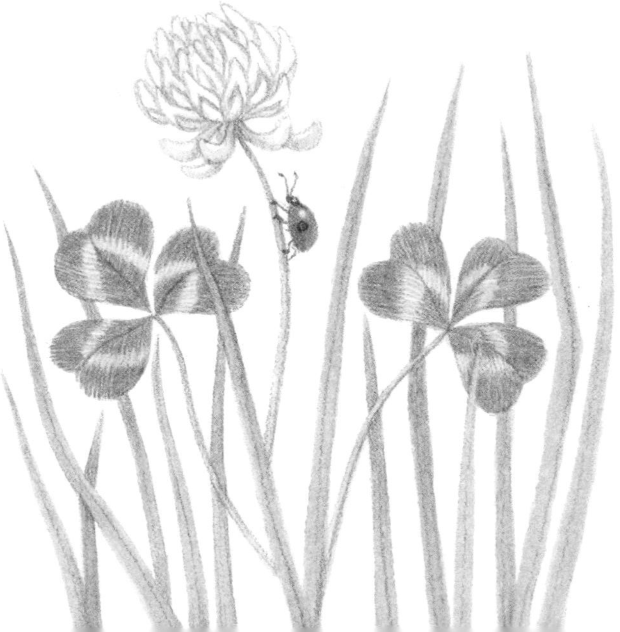

For Loveliness

Arthur L. Fischer

It has been said, and I agree,
That only God can make a tree;
He also can create a flower.
I saw one in a leafy bower
Beyond a trellised gate
And lingered, though the hour grew late.

Gazing there, quite undetected,
My eyes beheld the unexpected;
I did not see a scarlet rose,
Dramatic in its vivid pose,
Nor yet a peerless lily white
That with the dusk recedes from sight.

Ah no, imagine my surprise—
Forget-me-nots and summer skies.
As fragile as a crystal glass,
So delicate, this dainty lass.
With beaming, azure-tinted eyes,
Forget-me-nots and summer skies!

Like a great poet,
nature produces the greatest results
with the simplest means.
They are simply a sun,
flowers, water, and love.

—Heine

Forget-me-nots brighten a footpath in Vermont's Green Mountain National Forest. Photo by William H. Johnson/Johnson's Photography.

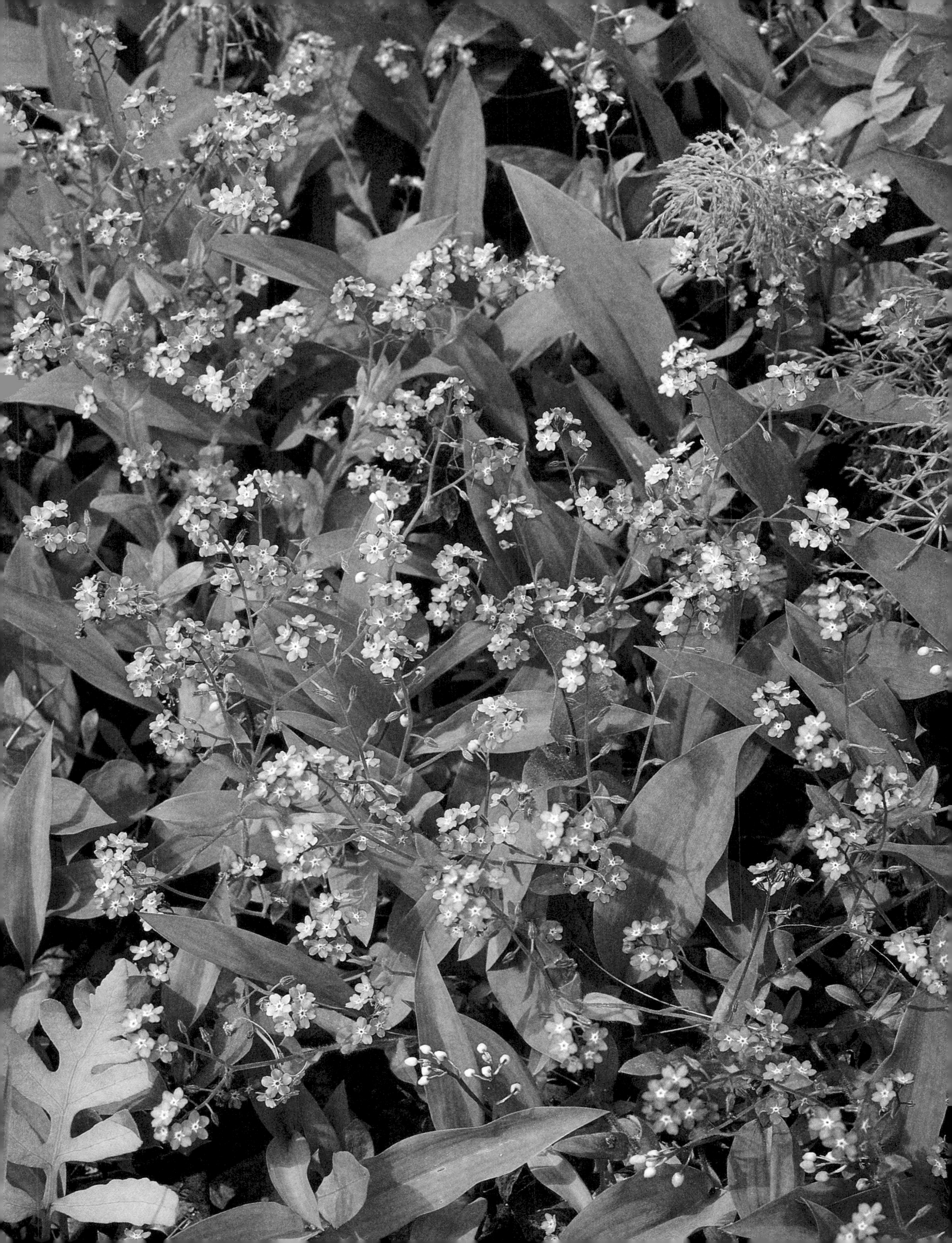

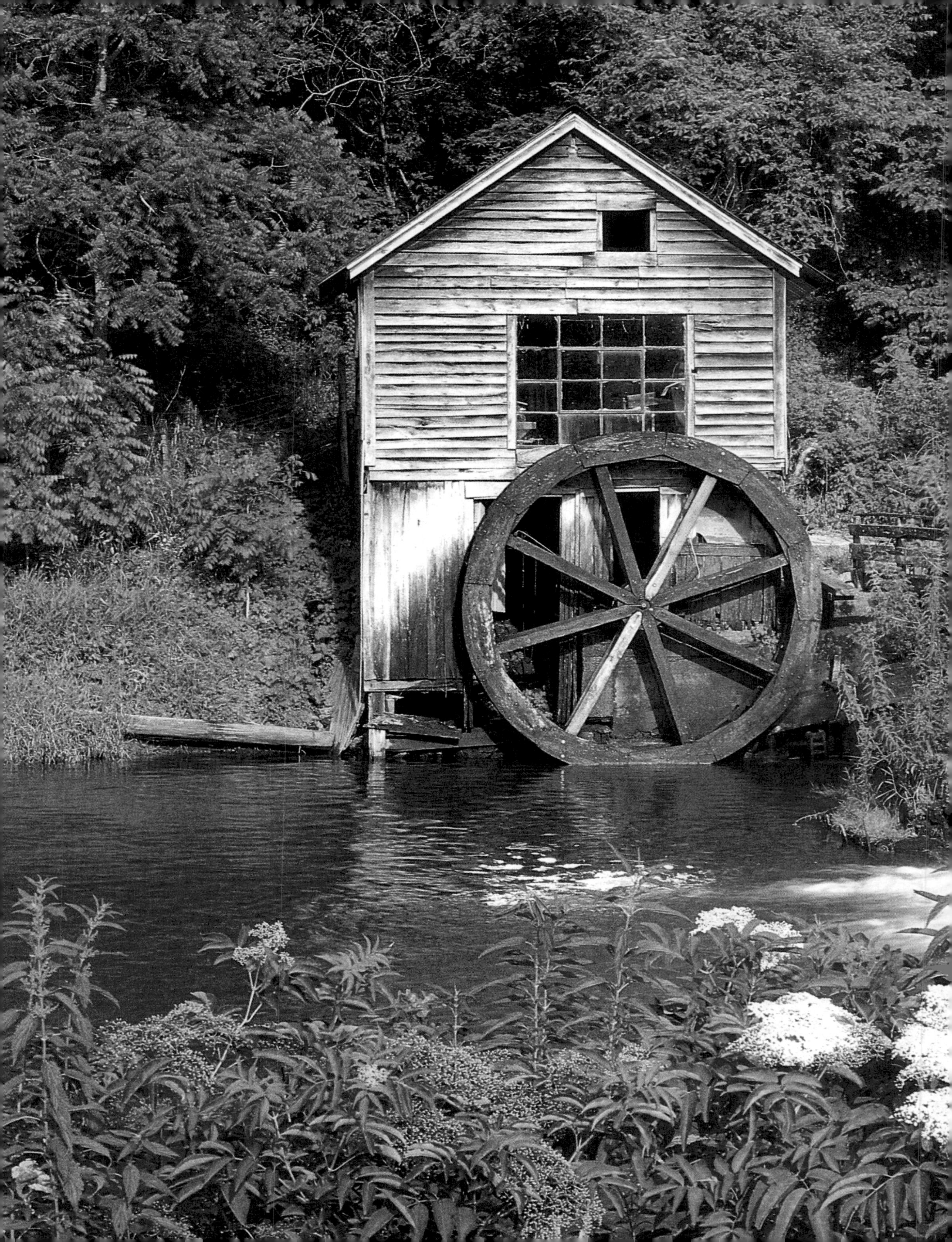

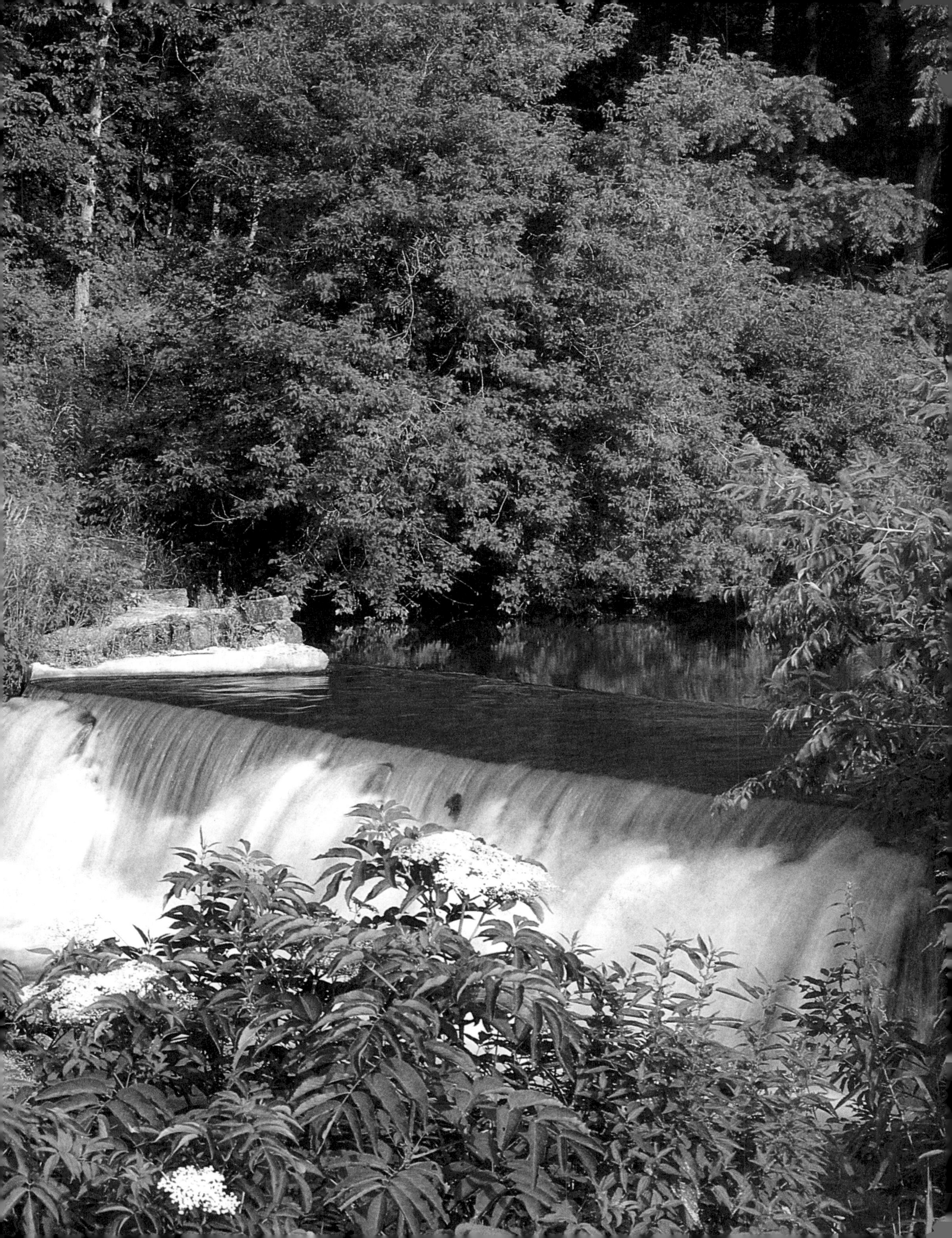

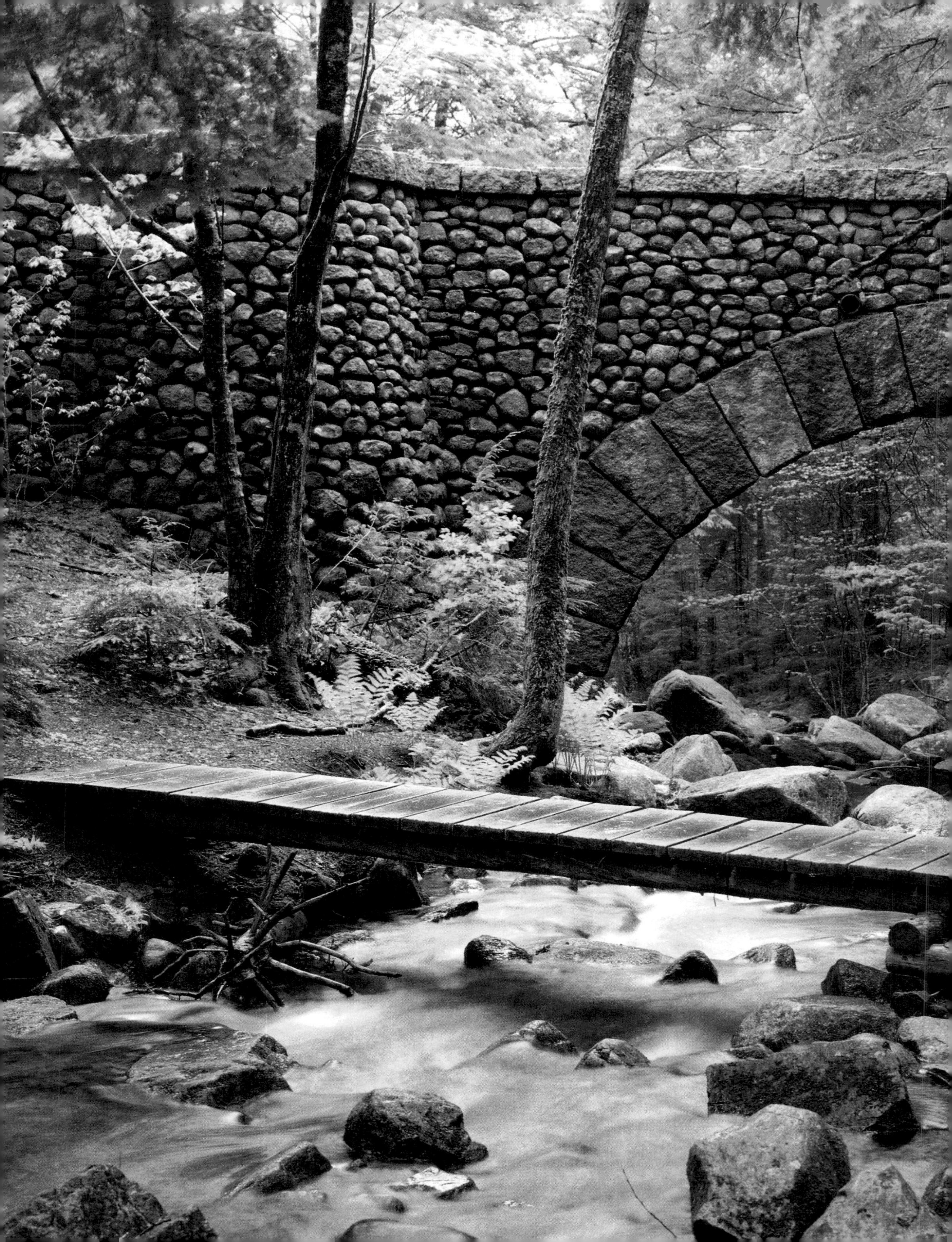

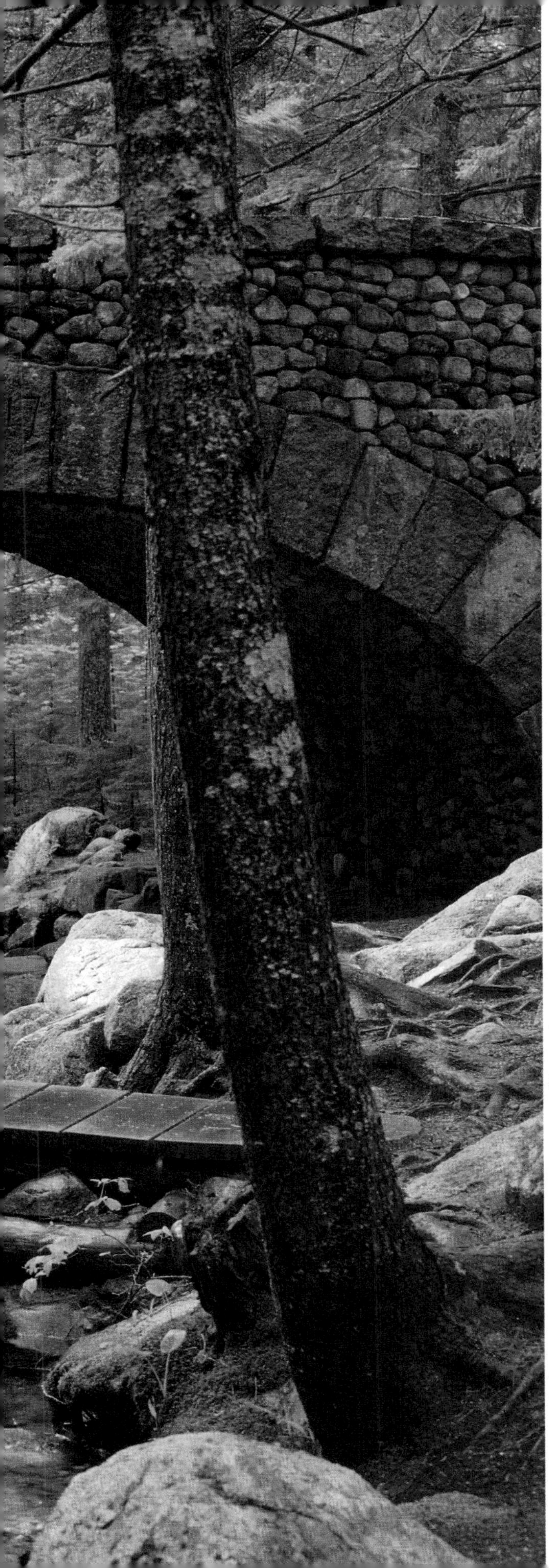

Winsome Songs of Summertime

Lon Myruski

I love to stroll the countryside
'Long summer's dirt-clad roads
Where wildings scamper in the care
Of wind-song chaperones.
And hidden high above in boughs
'Neath leafy camouflage,
Elusive songbirds improvise
Their musical montage.

A wooden bridge o'er sighing brook
Looms framed by azure skies;
Its creaking boards like bagpipes skirl
When trod by passers-by.
Then rustling forth on weathered rails
Sway verdant ivy skeins
Exchanging whispers with the wind—
Soft melodies unchained.

Afield, 'cross wayside meadows waft
Cicada chorusings
As orchestrating crickets pluck
Away at my heartstrings.
And here amid beguiling airs
I tarry the encore
Of winsome songs of summertime,
Beloved evermore.

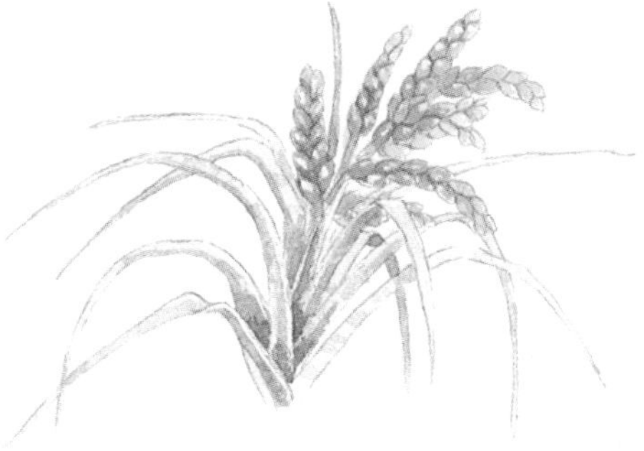

Overleaf photograph: Built in 1850, this stone dam at Hyde's Mill in Iowa County, Wisconsin, still stands strong. Photo by Darryl R. Beers.

Left: A cobblestone bridge shadows its wooden counterpart in the Acadia National Park in Maine. Photo by Gene Ahrens.

To Illustrate

Sylvia Trent Auxier

When my spouse sees upon the lawn
A spiderweb with dew thereon,
He writes its praises in a lyric
Which one might call a "panegyric."

But when, within our little house,
One brushes my poetic spouse,
The words he uses to describe
It then one calls a "diatribe."

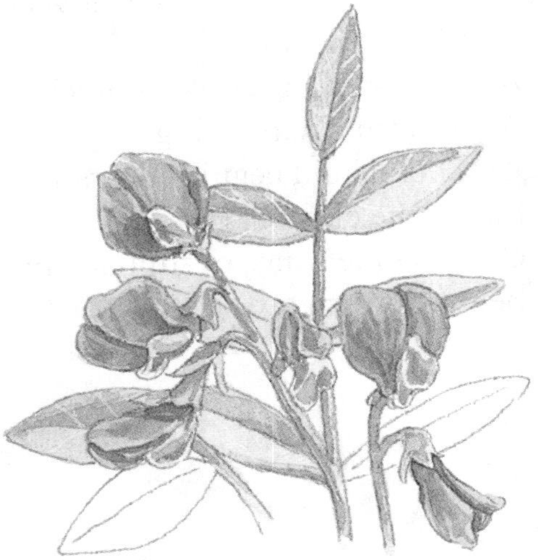

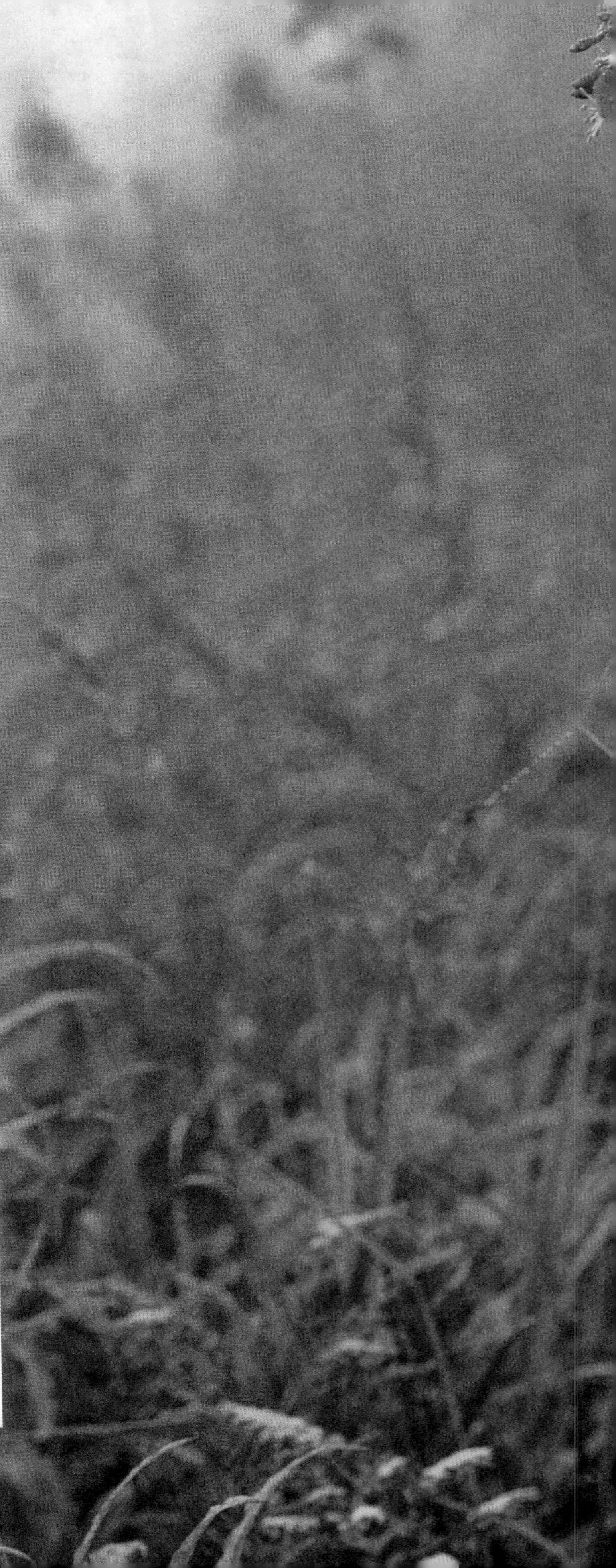

The morning dew sparkles on a spider's web among the fireweed in Lubec, Maine. Photo by Dick Dietrich.

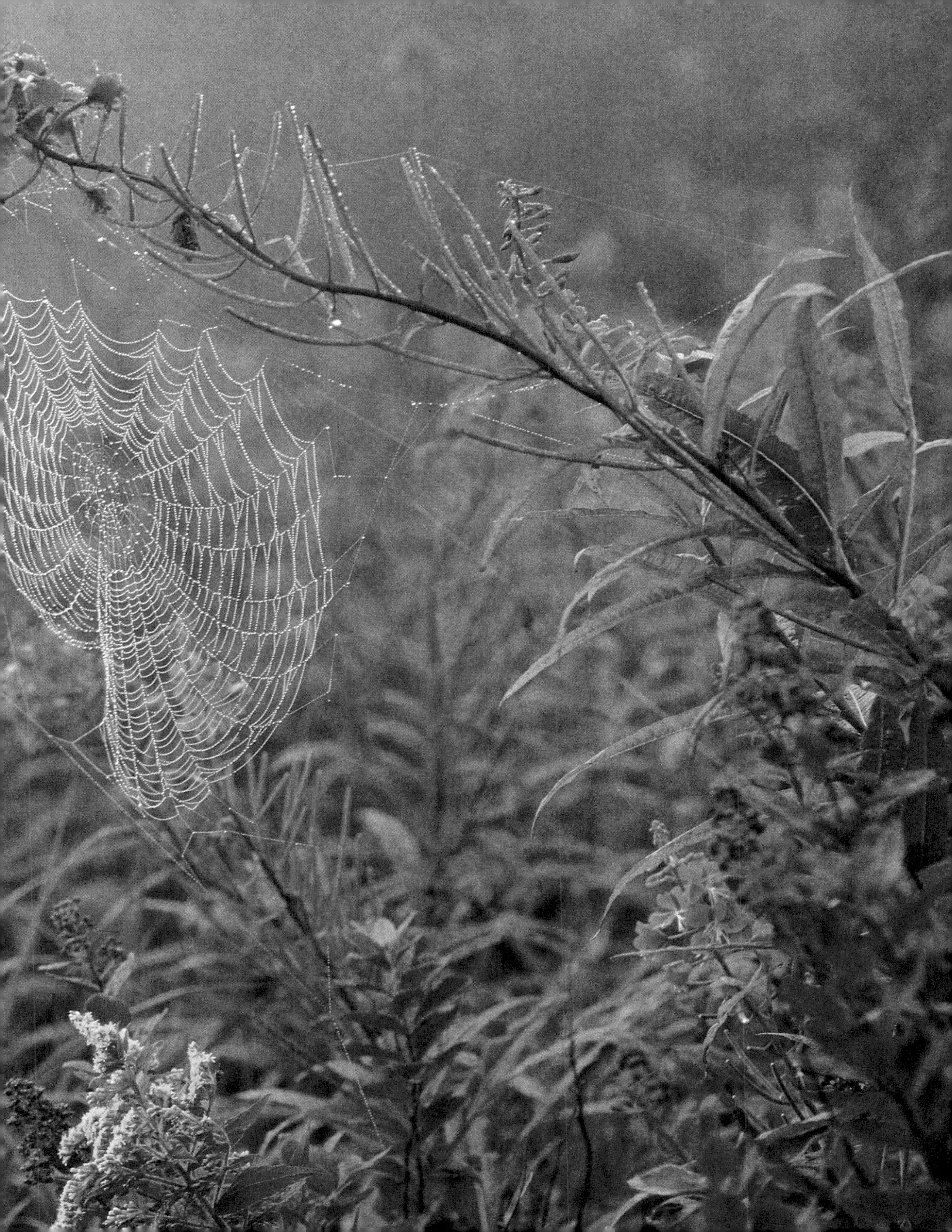

Readers' Reflections

Editor's Note: Readers are invited to submit unpublished, original poetry for possible publication in future issues of Ideals. *Please send typed copies only; manuscripts will not be returned. Writers receive $10 for each published submission. Send material to Readers' Reflections, Ideals Publications, Inc., P.O. Box 305300, Nashville, Tennessee 37230-5300.*

Sweet Summer Day

Vicky A. Luong
Maple Shade, New Jersey

Chattering birds greet the morning,
And the grass is kissed by the dew.
A summer day is unfolding,
And it is beckoning to you—
To a sunny-side-up afternoon
With baby blue skies out to play.
While everywhere fun is escaping—
It can't be held captive today.
After dinner, a storm rushes in
For a quick little how-do-you-do.
And a rainbow follows in colors
That seem too good to be true.
Then a bellowing breeze ushers in
The close of this sweet summer day.
And sundown sketches memories
That will never fade away!

I Called My Daddy Papa

Hazel Bell Nicholas
Marietta, Oklahoma

I called my daddy Papa;
In turn, he called me Son.
We plowed the fields together
From dawn to set of sun.

He taught the love of nature,
The smell of fresh-turned sod,
To till the soil and plant it
Then trust the yield to God.
He said that honest sweating
Would do a fellow good;
And as I walked behind him,
Somehow I knew it would.

Now when I see the turning
And smell the pungent smell,
I remember Papa planting;
And I'm lost in memory's spell.

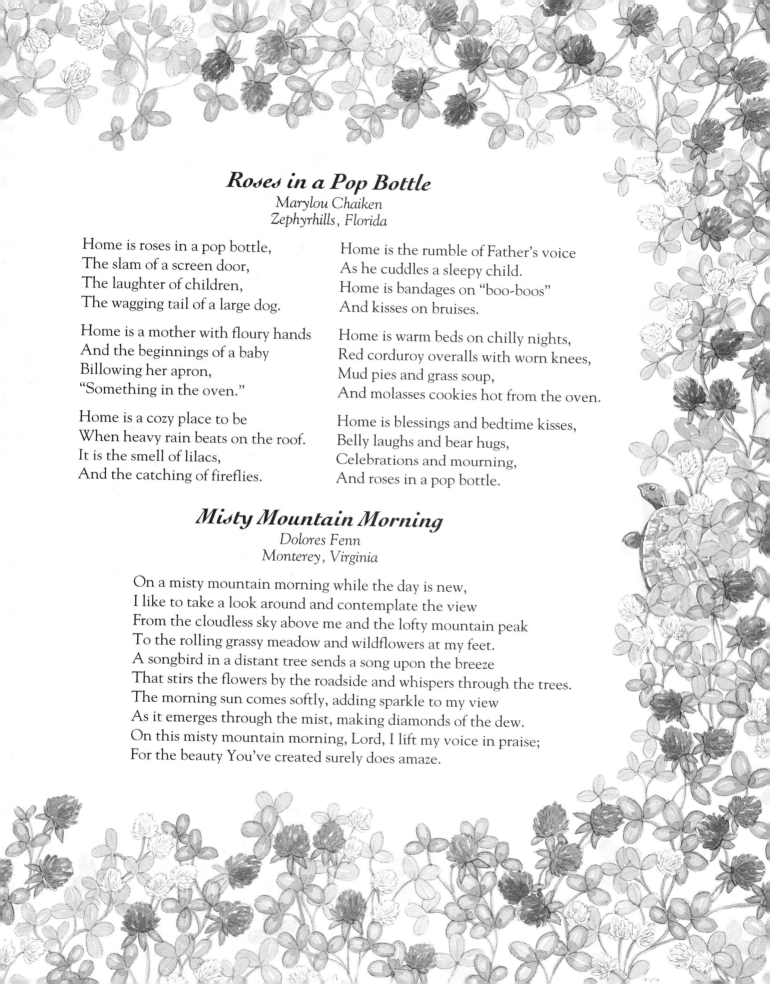

Roses in a Pop Bottle

Marylou Chaiken
Zephyrhills, Florida

Home is roses in a pop bottle,
The slam of a screen door,
The laughter of children,
The wagging tail of a large dog.

Home is a mother with floury hands
And the beginnings of a baby
Billowing her apron,
"Something in the oven."

Home is a cozy place to be
When heavy rain beats on the roof.
It is the smell of lilacs,
And the catching of fireflies.

Home is the rumble of Father's voice
As he cuddles a sleepy child.
Home is bandages on "boo-boos"
And kisses on bruises.

Home is warm beds on chilly nights,
Red corduroy overalls with worn knees,
Mud pies and grass soup,
And molasses cookies hot from the oven.

Home is blessings and bedtime kisses,
Belly laughs and bear hugs,
Celebrations and mourning,
And roses in a pop bottle.

Misty Mountain Morning

Dolores Fenn
Monterey, Virginia

On a misty mountain morning while the day is new,
I like to take a look around and contemplate the view
From the cloudless sky above me and the lofty mountain peak
To the rolling grassy meadow and wildflowers at my feet.
A songbird in a distant tree sends a song upon the breeze
That stirs the flowers by the roadside and whispers through the trees.
The morning sun comes softly, adding sparkle to my view
As it emerges through the mist, making diamonds of the dew.
On this misty mountain morning, Lord, I lift my voice in praise;
For the beauty You've created surely does amaze.

AND NEVER KNEW

Jessie Wilmore Murton

The milkman left a bottle of milk—
But there was more: he left cows of silk—
Though of course the milkman couldn't know—
With fields of clover, and buckwheat snow;
And rolling meadows of green and gold,
By a rambling barn, long gray and old,
Where an apple-cheeked boy, from an ancient mow,
Threw down fresh hay for a soft-eyed cow.

And he left mornings of silvered rose,
And the feel of dew on bare brown toes,
With pasture bars for a boy to climb;
And a shadowy moon, at evening time.
He left a bottle—as milkmen do—
With rattle and bang; and never knew
That he left childhood, and freckles, and tan
Of a country boy—to a city man!

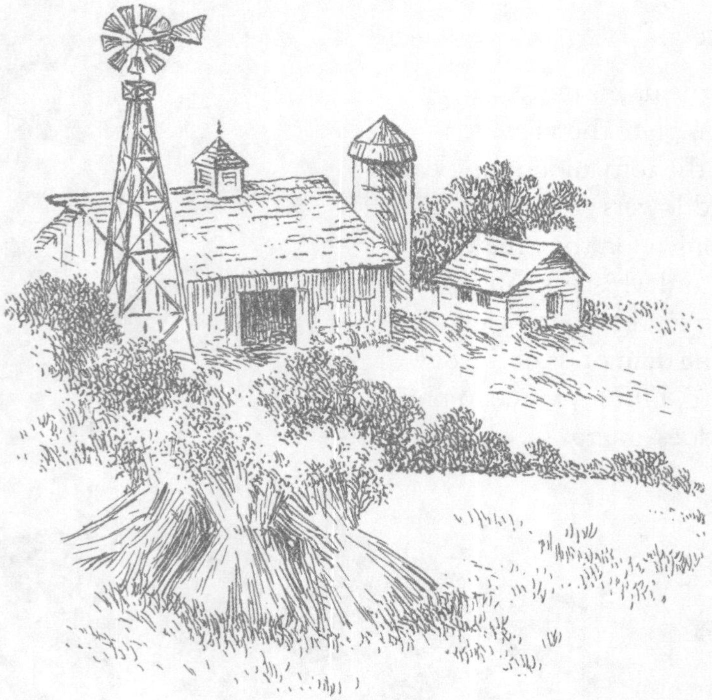

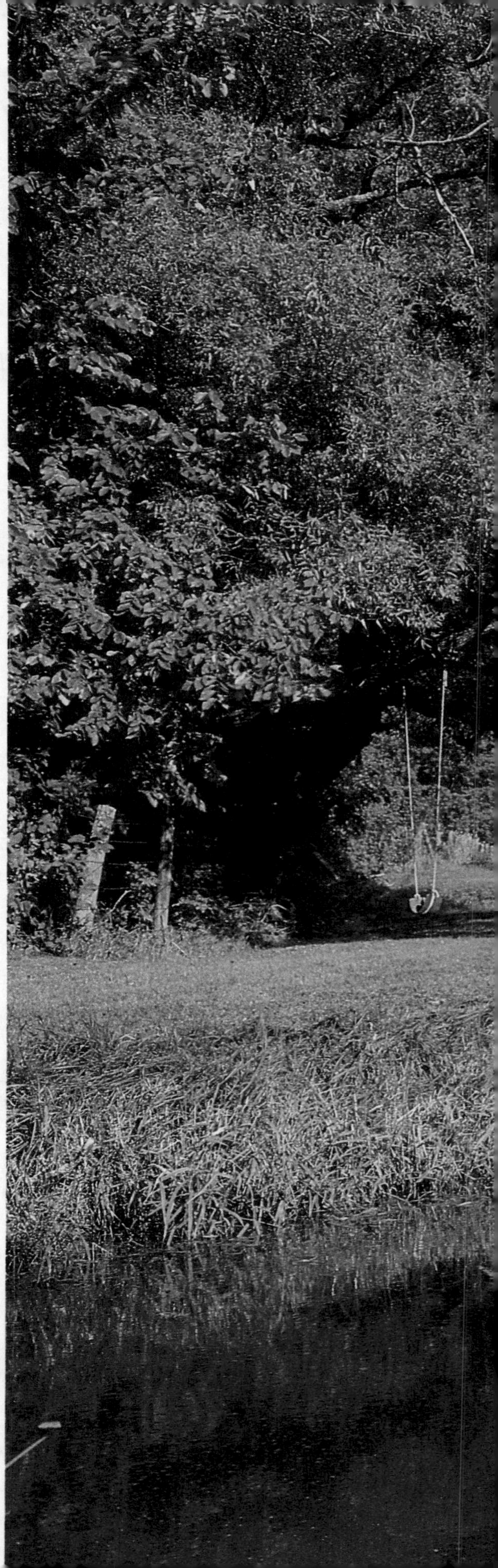

A perfect day in the country is captured in this photo of Fond du Lac County, Wisconsin, taken by Darryl R. Beers.

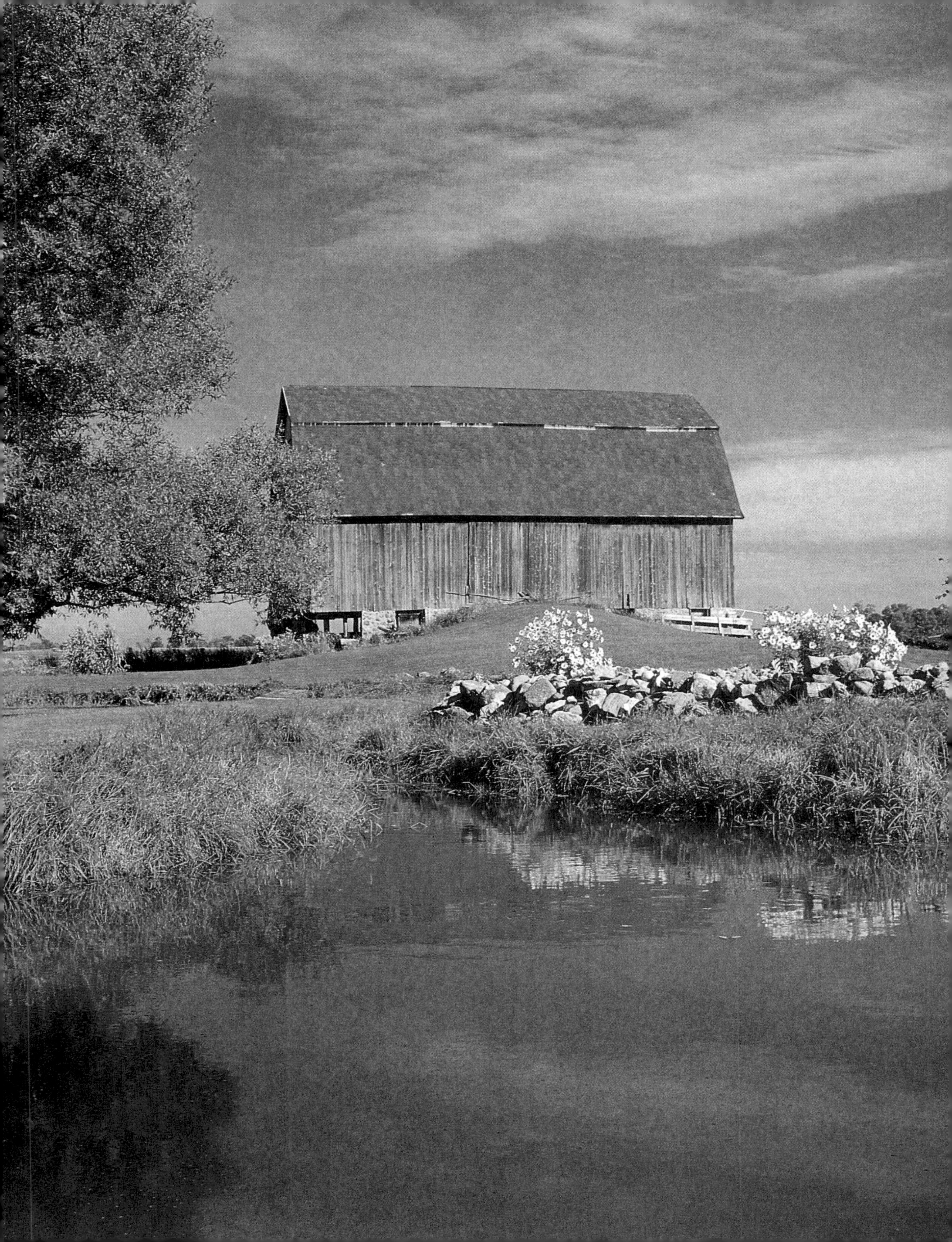

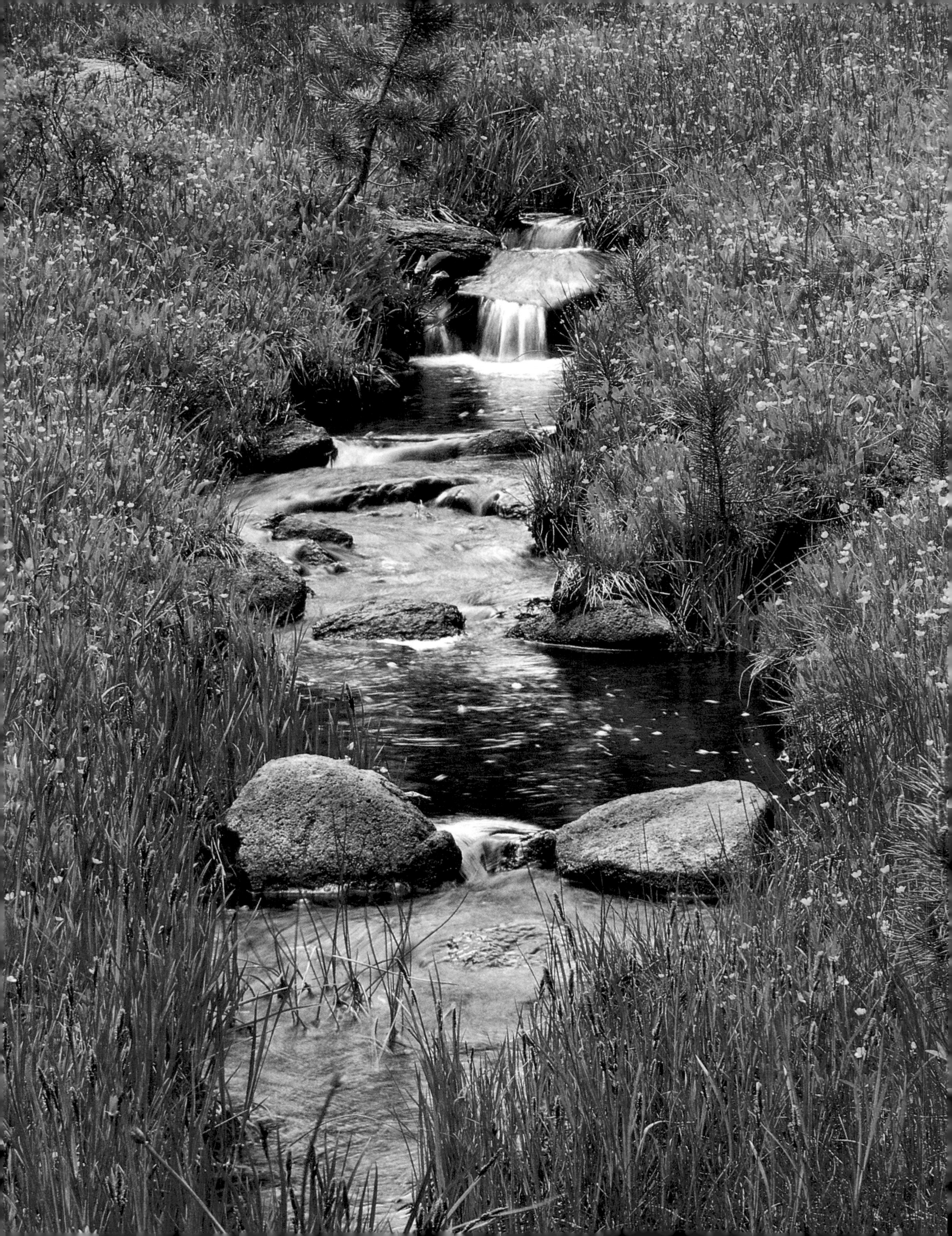

A SKIPPER OF STONES

I have a yearning sometimes to be back again by the Bozenkill and its waterfalls in Upstate New York. I still dream of the rushing waters that come in summer downpours or in autumn's heavy rains. I often remember the water's murmuring lullaby in winter and the crushing breakup of the ice in spring.

But it is the summer Bozenkill I am dreaming of today, and the boy who so often followed the winding stream and skipped stones across the surface of its quiet pools. The summer creek was almost always a gentle one, created of only miniature streams trickling down over the protruding rock and shale of the falls.

As a boy, I often followed the Bozenkill just to enjoy the art of skipping small, flat stones over the pools. I would watch them rise and dip and rise again until disappearing at last below the surface of the water, leaving ripples that reached out to touch the arms of the shore. Now I sometimes compare those skipping stones, rising and dipping, to the undulating flight of the goldfinch flying over the nearby pasture, rich in its patches of thistles and weeds.

I still skip stones when I come upon a brook during my walks in the foothills of the Blue Ridge. And I still dream. I wonder if the dreams are anything like the ones I used to have. Perhaps there is still enough of the barefoot boy of long ago left in the dreams of a man of today.

No matter what the dreams, of a boy or a man, I still like to be a skipper of stones over the surface of summer's quiet pools.

The author of two published books, Lansing Christman has been contributing to Ideals *for more than twenty years. Mr. Christman has also been published in several American, foreign, and braille anthologies. He lives in rural South Carolina.*

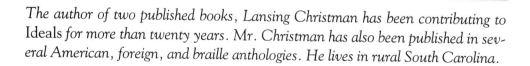

A stream in Oregon's Mount Hood National Forest is framed by wildflowers. Photo by Wayne Aldridge/International Stock.

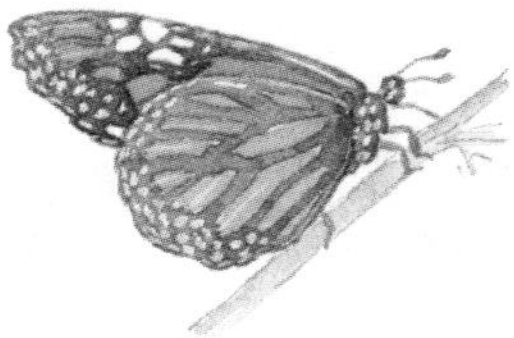

THE DESERTED PASTURE

Bliss Carman

I love the stony pasture
That no one else will have.
The old gray rocks so friendly seen,
So durable and brave.

In tranquil contemplation
It watches through the year,
Seeing the frosty stars arise,
The slender moons appear.

Its music is the rain-wind,
Its choristers the birds,
And there are secrets in its heart
Too wonderful for words.

It keeps the bright-eyed creatures
That play about its walls,
Though long ago its milking herds
Were banished from their stalls.

Only the children come there,
For buttercups in May,
Or nuts in autumn, where it lies
Dreaming the hours away.

Long since its strength was given
To making good increase,
And now its soul is turned again
To beauty and to peace.

There in the early springtime
The violets are blue,
And adder-tongues in coats of gold
Are garmented anew.

There bayberry and aster
Are crowded on its floors,
When marching summer halts to praise
The Lord of out-of-doors.

And there October passes
In gorgeous livery—
In purple ash, and crimson oak,
And golden tulip tree.

And when the winds of winter
Their bugle blasts begin,
The snowy hosts of heaven arrive
And pitch their tents therein.

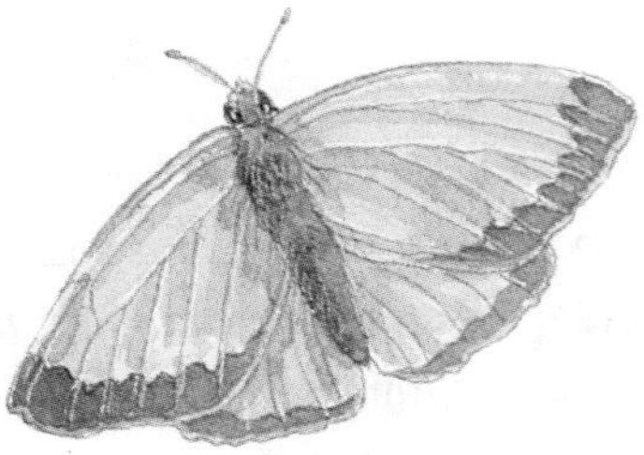

Summer wildflowers edge a fenced pasture in Ohio's Big Wood River Valley. Photo by Jeff Gnass.

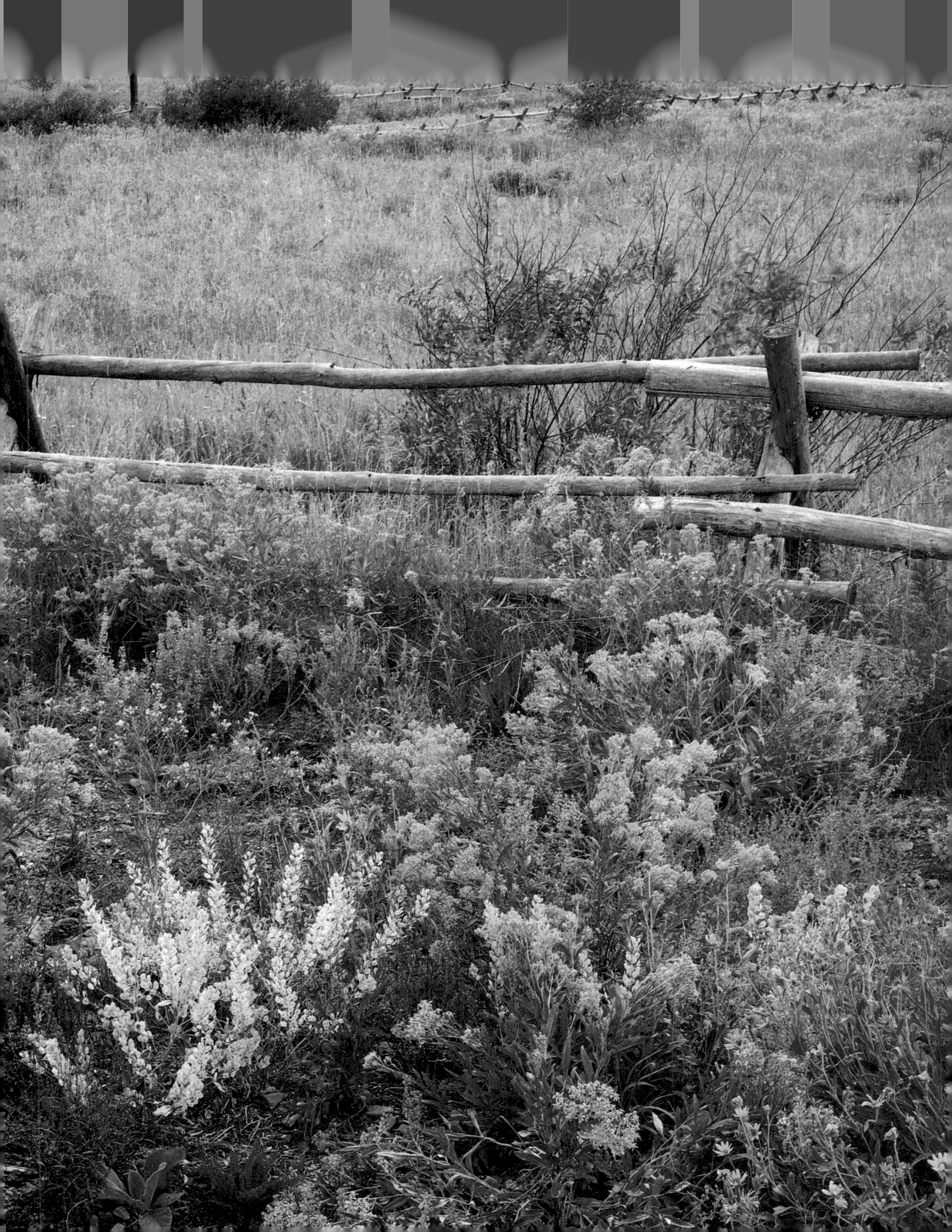

From My Garden Journal

Deana Deck

CONEFLOWERS

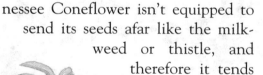

The first coneflower I ever encountered was an endangered one: the Tennessee Coneflower. I was on a wildflower hike with friends when we entered a small sunny meadow from a wooded glade. There before us was a beautiful patch of rosy-purple blooms. I immediately imagined this flower spreading its color throughout my backyard, so I was disappointed when our hike leader pointed out that this particular coneflower is endangered and grows in only four places in the state. For centuries the Tennessee Coneflower has grown wild in the open woods throughout the state, but the development of more and more land has threatened this lovely little plant. The Tennessee Coneflower isn't equipped to send its seeds afar like the milkweed or thistle, and therefore it tends to grow primarily in clumps and in one location.

Although I was disappointed that I couldn't just drive to my local garden center and purchase a flat of Tennessee Coneflowers, I was thrilled to discover that several other varieties of coneflower are readily available; and I soon found a cultivated version in a gardening catalog. Most coneflower species are hardier and more widespread than the Tennessee variety, and many of them have been hybridized, resulting in modified color and blossom shape.

The name coneflower is derived from the shape of the blossom, which resembles a badminton shuttlecock. The dark red, cone-shaped center of the flower is surrounded by daisy-like rays or petals ranging in color from a deep rose shade to pale lavender. The distinctive shape and color of the coneflower made the plant easy to spot by Native Americans trailing the great buffalo herds across the Midwest prairies, where the purple coneflower grows wild. These nomadic hunters (who often used wild plants for food or medicine) used the coneflower's thick roots to make medicines.

Years later, as wagon trains began heading west, they rolled through the tall native grasses where the purple coneflower bloomed among the other prairie plants. The blooms joined the other native midwestern plants that were dug up and transplanted by settlers who were homesick for their colorful gardens back east.

Luckily, it's not necessary to dig up wildflowers to enjoy the beauty and ease of care of the coneflower today. The purple coneflower (*Echinacea purpurea*) is now the best known of nine species of coneflower. And for generations, breeders have been at work creating new varieties of lavender-pink beauties that can appear in gardens all across the country. Some cultivars, like Magnus, have a flatter, more daisy-like appearance. Bright Star and Crimson Star are other popular cultivars in the pink and purple color range, and White Swan is a dazzling white version of the same flower.

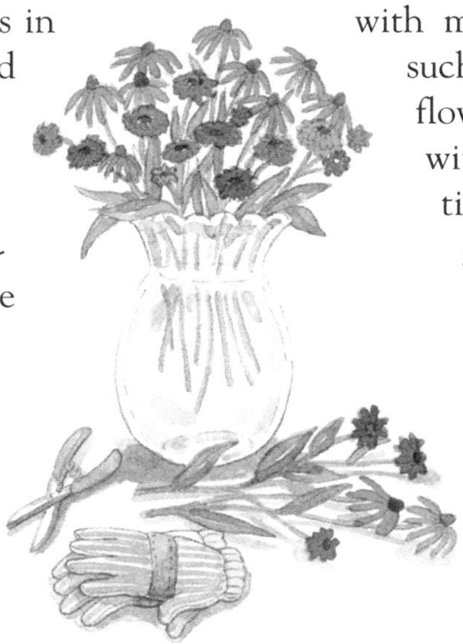

One of the nicest things about all these coneflowers is you can simply plant them and forget them. Like any plant, they appreciate a little food and water and demand full sunlight; but they aren't fussy about soil, and they seem to thrive in hot, dry summer weather. I've grown them for years and have never seen a bug chewing on them, although they easily attract butterflies which come to sip the nectar. The plants even seem to be immune to blight, fungal infections, powdery mildew, and other problems that are common in perennial gardens.

Once the coneflower begins blooming in early June, it won't stop until late September. That lengthy blooming period provides ample time to create indoor bouquets.

Coneflowers look best planted in large groupings where the clumps of individual plants can create a sensational summer display. Unlike many clump-forming perennials, they do not really need to be divided and, in fact, seem to prefer being left alone. Division is one way of propagating them, however, but root cuttings are just as effective (take the cutting in the fall). You can also let the flowerheads go to seed and scatter the seeds around the bed in the fall to increase the tribe.

Once the coneflower begins blooming in early June, it won't stop until late September. That lengthy blooming period provides ample time to create indoor bouquets; and as a cut flower, nothing outdoes the coneflower for longevity. It can remain attractive in a vase for as long as two weeks and blends beautifully with most other bright summer blooms such as zinnias. Even after your coneflowers stop blooming and the petals wither, the seed heads remain attractive in the garden and attract hungry goldfinches in winter.

The coneflower might be the perfect plant: a garden perennial immune to bugs and disease that blooms nonstop all summer, feeds birds in the winter, and re-blooms without a fuss every year. With all their positive characteristics, the common varieties of coneflowers (unlike the Tennessee Coneflower) are surely safe from any threat of endangerment, and I'm definitely glad. A colorful patch of coneflowers is definitely a pleasant discovery on a nature walk, but sometimes the best place for a walk is my own backyard.

Deana Deck tends to her flowers, plants, and vegetables at her home in Nashville, Tennessee, where her popular garden column is a regular feature in The Tennessean.

Dinah Kneading Dough

Paul Laurence Dunbar

I have seen full many a sight
Born of day or drawn by night:
Sunlight on a silver stream,
Golden lilies all a-dream,
Lofty mountains, bold and proud,
Veiled beneath the lacelike cloud;
But no lovely sight I know
Equals Dinah kneading dough.

Brown arms buried elbow-deep
Their domestic rhythm keep,
As with steady sweep they go
Through the gently yielding dough.
Maids may vaunt their finer charms—
Naught to me like Dinah's arms;
Girls may draw, or paint, or sew—
I love Dinah kneading dough.

Eyes of jet and teeth of pearl,
Hair, some say, too tight a-curl;
But the dainty maid I deem
Very near perfection's dream.
Swift she works, and only flings
Me a glance—the least of things.
And I wonder, does she know
That my heart is in the dough?

This country kitchen reflects the charm of a restored nineteenth-century home. Photo by Jessie Walker.

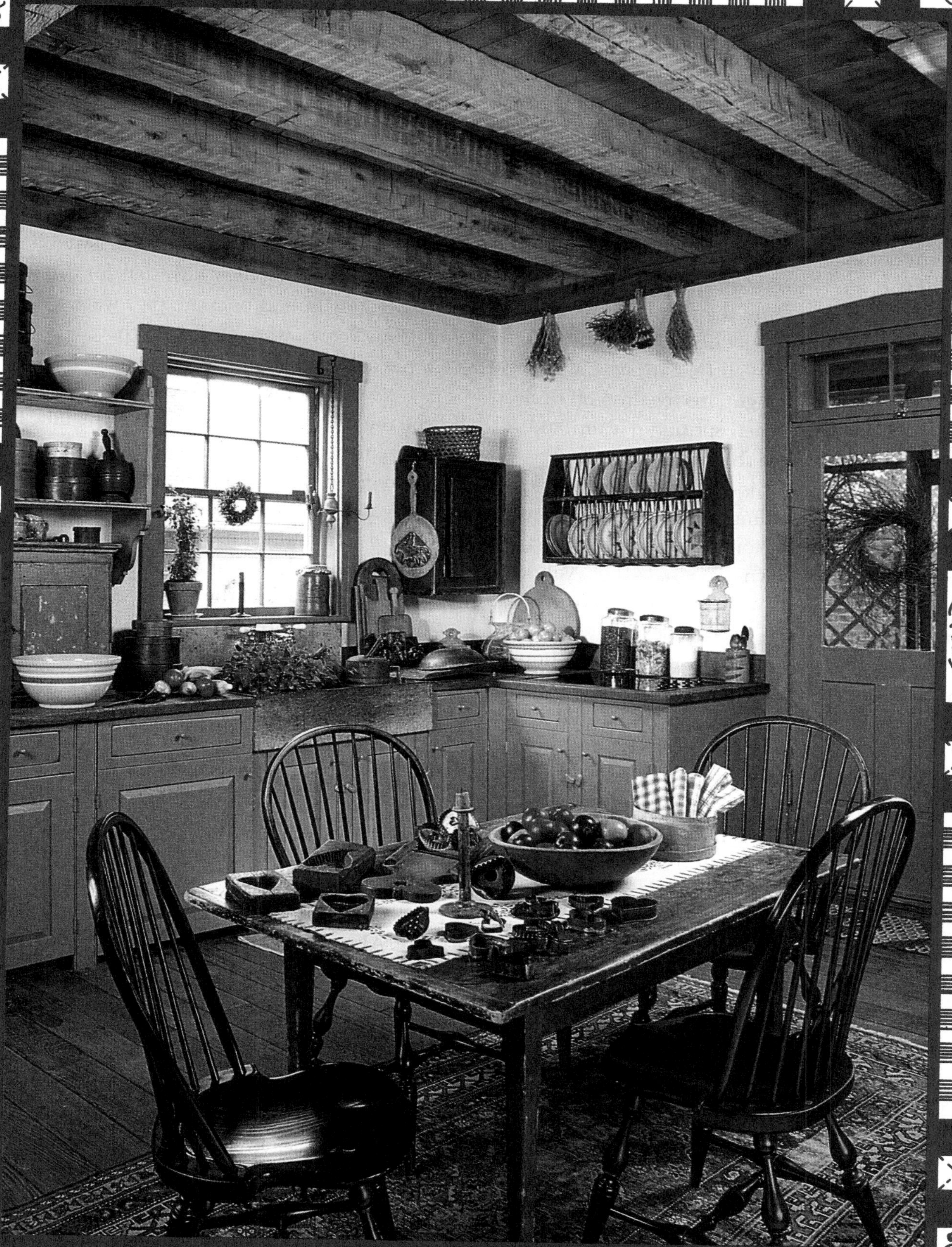

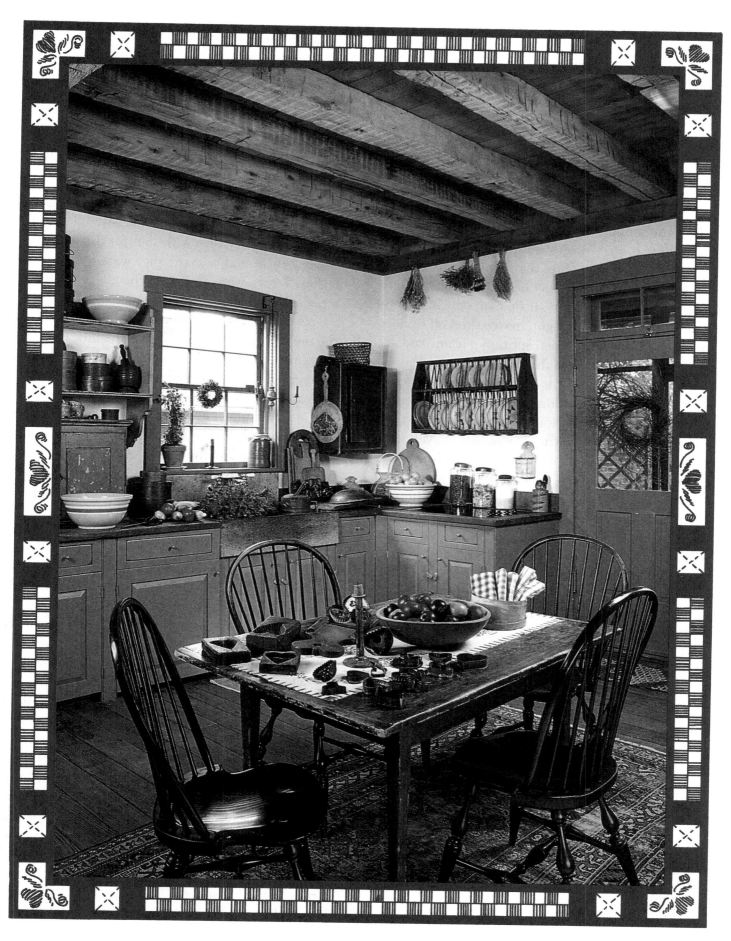

THE PICNIC TO THE HILLS

Edna Jaques

The picnic to the hills was the highlight of the summer. We always held it on the first of July. It was the only outing of the year.

I couldn't sleep a wink the night before; I would just lie there in bed with my little sister, getting up a dozen times to look out the little narrow window and see if it were getting daylight, maybe drop off to sleep for a few minutes and then spring up again and see dawn coming up across the flats. And there is no more glorious sight on this earth than the sun slowly rising on the prairie, filling the summer world with colors that defy description. First a faint pink, then the full blooming of dawn—green, orange, yellow— and always that sense of wonder at the vastness of the earth from rim to rim—empty and silent, yet filled with a strange breathing like wings above the house.

Meadowlarks would be piping their songs, hundreds of them. The rooster would let out a few squawks; the dog would shake himself and wander towards the barn, as if to reassure himself that all was well; the hens would come out of the hen house door, ruffling their wings, and start to hunt for food. The old cow on her tether would rise and stretch and start to eat as if to say, "Well, get up everyone. It's another day."

By this time we three girls would be dressed. There were no "outfits" for us, just nice little print dresses, the good ones we had been saving for the occasion. We could hear Dad in the kitchen making the fire . . . and yelling at Maw to hurry.

Breakfast would be a hurried meal: good oatmeal porridge, big slices of homemade bread with syrup, and homemade butter. Dad and the boys would each eat a big slice of fried pork. Maw would have her tea; there was no tea for kids in those days, just milk or water gulped down in a hurry for fear we'd miss something.

Water would be left in pans in the yard for the chickens; the milk would be strained and set in blue pans in the cellar; the mother hens were left in their little overnight houses with slats for the little chickens to run in and out; the pigs were fed with extra rations; cows were freshly tethered on their long ropes and horses were fed.

My mother would have made most of the lunch the night before and packed it in the blue bread pan: homemade headcheese, potato salad, radishes and little green onions, and maybe . . . a raisin pie, and her good homemade cookies.

Old Kit and Farmer would be hitched to the lumber wagon with Dad and Maw on the spring seat, we three in the back of the wagon as usual, laughing and wild with excitement. As the hills would loom nearer, we would see a few trees, our first glimpse of them since the picnic the year before.

The trail headed due south, winding here and there with a little curve around a gopher or badger hole, past Gallaugher's, Fraser's, Espelein's, where there was a tiny coulee to cross. Dad would ease the horses down the little bank and splash through the creek, maybe two feet of water in it, and then up the far bank, the horses flopping and scrambling for a foothold as if we were crossing the river Jordan.

Ahead, the hills would beckon, rising blue and lovely against the sky; the horses would trot along quietly as if they too were enjoying the break from the monotonous prairie and the plow.

My two brothers, Bruce and Clyde, would ride their horses; no wagon for them. Now and then they would pass us at a gallop, then circle back and race away again, leaving a little cloud of dust that settled down on the sage bushes and short grass, described by the oldtimers as "prairie wool."

Our destination would be "old Buchanan's ranch," exactly twelve miles south of our homestead. He would come out to meet us with his dog, smiling

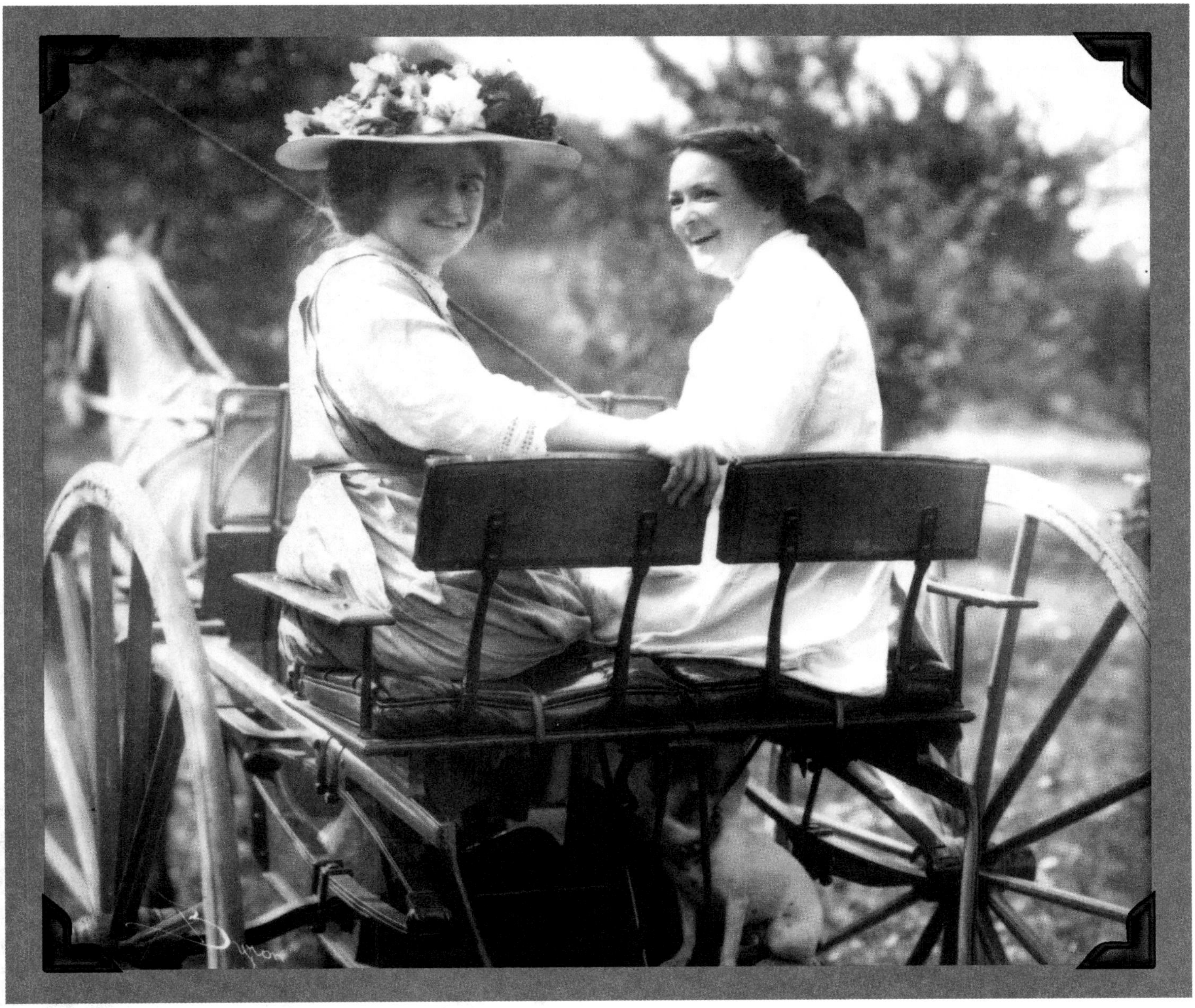

As two friends head off to a picnic in their horse-drawn cart, their dog sneaks along for the ride. Photo by FPG.

and glad to see another human being, I suppose.

The ranch cattle and horses, hearing us come, would get on top of the hill behind the house and view us from afar, half afraid. There were trees there, real trees that we only saw once a year. . . . We kids would run up and down the little hills, tripping and falling and wild with joy just to be able to run up a hill. We'd take a drink of water from "Buchanan's spring," which was known all over the country as being the sweetest water on earth. How good it was. . . .

For the first year or so there would be just us and two or three other families, but soon more settlers would join in; and within five or six years there would be maybe fifty people out. Not many, I know, but fifty people in a new country was wonderful. The women would talk and laugh and compare notes on setting hens and new calves, and discuss how good it was to get out and talk to someone besides themselves.

Then it would be time to "hit for home" in the blue dusk of day, everyone quieter; we three kids in the back of the wagon were happy too, to be going home.

Toots, the dog, would come out to meet us, smiling . . . to see us back. The house and barn looked strangely comfortable in the quiet dusk—the cows waiting to be milked, the hens to be fed and their water pans filled up again. Then quietness would settle down and fold us in, as if the earth too was glad we were home safe and sound.

RUSTIC TREASURES

Vida Primm

Not far out from the county seat,
The homestead lay in peaceful scene
Mid widespread fields of golden wheat
And pastures lush with summer's green.

The winding road went up the ridge
And wandered by the old rail fence
Then through the rustic covered bridge
Into a timber dark and dense.

The chimney top came into view
Beyond the barn and water tank,
Across the brook where cattails grew
Beside the green and grassy bank.

The iron pump and dinner bell
Bade threshing crews to come inside
And, oh, what happy tales they'd tell
Of Grandma's table, set with pride.

The kitchen range prepared the best
In slow-baked beans and homemade bread.
Her country ham withstood the test—
That's how she kept her family fed.

Those happy tunes we used to sing,
The organ playing soft and low,
And Grandpa telling tales of kings—
Our life was simple long ago.

Evening light falls over a farm on Whidby Island in Washington.
Photo by Terry Donnelly.

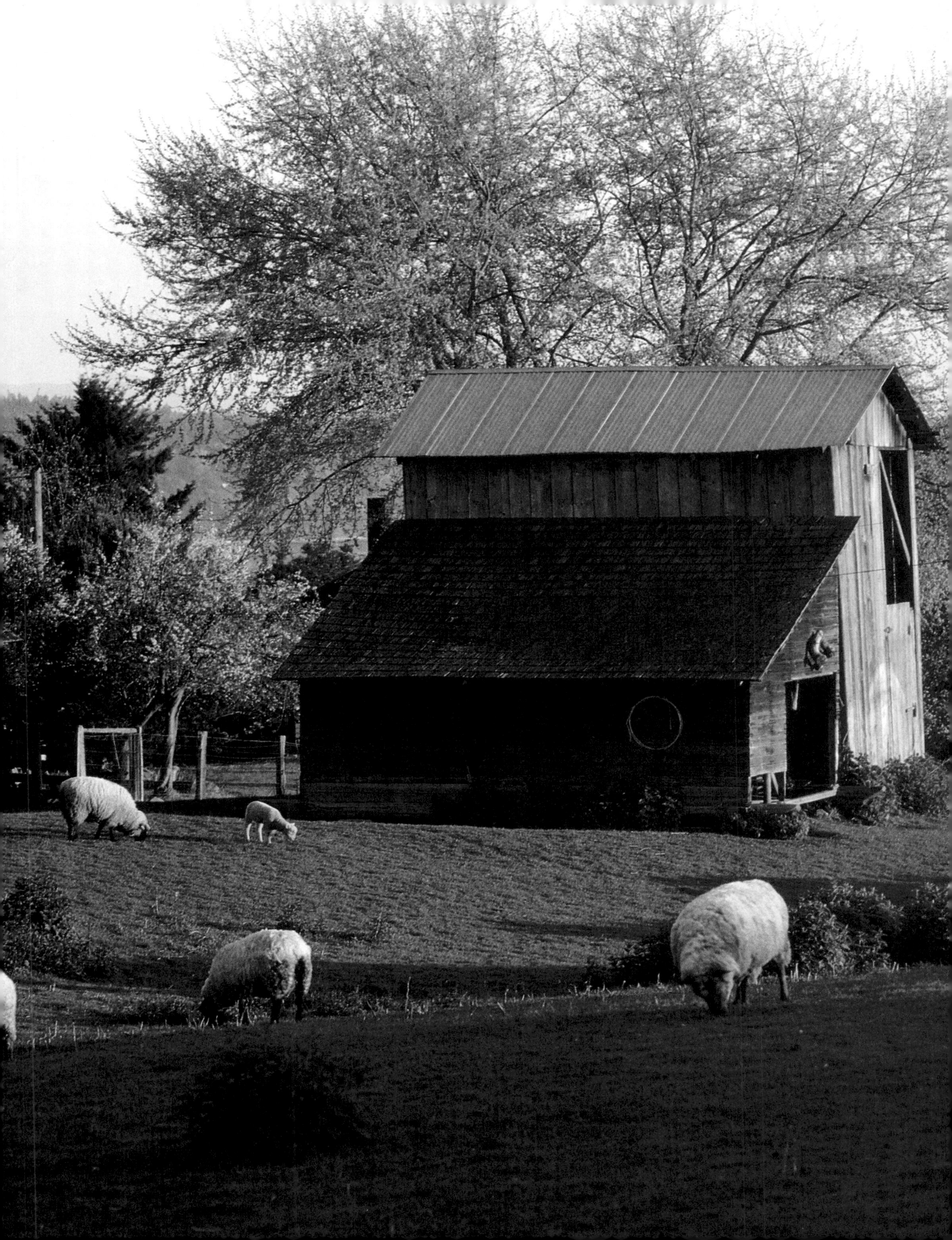

Ideals' Family Recipes

Throughout the summer, backyards across the nation become hosts to many a barbecue, complete with homemade food cooked right on the grill. Be sure to eat the chicken and the corn with your hands — licking your fingers is part of the fun. We would love to try your best-loved recipe too. Mail a typed copy of the recipe along with your name, address, and phone number to Ideals Magazine, ATTN: Recipes, P.O. Box 305300, Nashville, Tennessee 37230. *We will pay $10 for each recipe used.*

Picnic Chicken
Joann Taylor of Aubrey, Texas

1   8-ounce can crushed pineapple with juice
¼   cup Teriyaki sauce
2   tablespoons lemon juice
2   tablespoons red wine vinegar
2   cloves crushed garlic
1   tablespoon olive oil
¼   teaspoon mesquite liquid smoke (optional)
6   skinless, boneless chicken breasts

In a shallow dish, combine first 7 ingredients. Mix well; add chicken, turning once. Cover and chill 1 to 2 hours, turning occasionally. Remove chicken from marinade and place on grill. Cover the grill and cook chicken over medium coals (300° F to 400° F) 5 to 6 minutes on each side. Makes 6 servings.

Grilled Fruit Kabobs with Citrus Sauce
Mrs. Susan Murphy of Eugene, Oregon

1   8-ounce container vanilla yogurt
¼   cup honey, divided
2   tablespoons orange juice
1   teaspoon grated orange peel
½   teaspoon grated lemon peel
4   cups fresh fruit pieces (pineapple wedges, whole strawberries, nectarine and kiwi chunks)
16   1-inch cubes pound cake (approximately one half loaf)
2   tablespoons melted butter

In a small bowl, blend yogurt, 2 tablespoons of the honey, orange juice, and orange and lemon peels; cover and refrigerate until serving time. Soak eight 10-inch wooden skewers in water 30 minutes. Alternately thread fruit pieces and pound cake on skewers. In a small bowl, combine butter and remaining honey; mix well. Grill kabobs directly above heat source 8 to 10 minutes or until cake is toasted, turning and brushing with butter and honey mixture frequently. Serve immediately with citrus sauce. Makes 8 kabobs.

Summer Cole Slaw

Lydia Busick of Columbia City, Indiana

2 cups granulated sugar
½ cup vinegar
½ cup water
1 teaspoon celery seed
2 teaspoons mustard seed

2 teaspoons salt
1 large head cabbage (2 to 3 pounds)
3 medium onions
1 bunch celery
1 green pepper

In a medium bowl, combine sugar, vinegar, water, celery seed, mustard seed, and salt. Mix well; set aside. Roughly chop cabbage, onions, celery, and green pepper. Place in large bowl and stir together. Stir dressing, then pour over vegetables and mix well. Refrigerate overnight. Makes approximately 16 servings.

Roasted Corn

Pam Guy of Mattoon, Illinois

6 ears corn with husks

Pull down husks without removing. Remove silks; pull husks back into place to cover corn. Tie with cooking twine. Soak corn in cool water 10 minutes, drain. Place corn directly on grill (or in 375° F oven) 25 to 30 minutes, turning occasionally. Makes 6 servings.

Dill Beans

Carol Brown of Clyde, Texas

7 14½-ounce cans whole green beans, do not drain
2 tablespoons bacon drippings
1½ teaspoons dill seed
6 teaspoons butter
6 teaspoons all-purpose flour

1½ cups half and half
3 tablespoons grated onion
1 teaspoon cracked black pepper
   Dash of hot sauce
½ cup crushed butter-flavored crackers

In a large saucepan, place beans, bacon drippings, and dill seed. Bring to a boil; reduce heat and simmer 1½ hours. Remove from heat; refrigerate overnight.

Preheat oven to 350° F. Saving 1 cup of juice, place beans in colander to drain. Melt butter in a large saucepan over medium heat. Add flour and stir well. Add bean juice and half-and-half; stir well. Cook over medium heat until mixture thickens. Add onion, pepper, hot sauce, and beans; mix well. Transfer mixture to 1½-quart baking dish. Cover with cracker crumbs and bake 20 minutes. Makes approximately 14 servings.

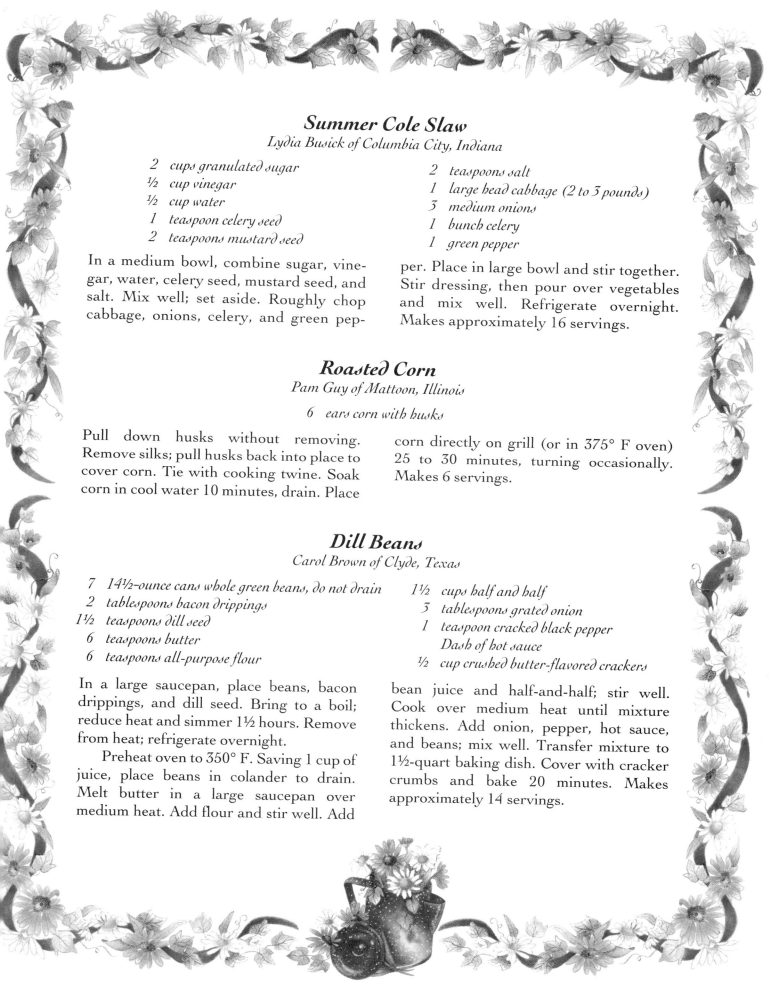

LITTLE COUNTRY CHURCH

Ellen Rebecca Fenn

It stands beside a crossroad on a knoll;
A symbol of the faith that lives inside
The heart of every man who enters there
For peace in troubled times and to abide
In reverent quietness. The open door
Is wide. It beckons with a waving hand,
A welcome staff to those with searching mind
Or questing heart which lacks its own command.
The scripture falls on eager, listening ear;
Abiding faith is voiced by hymnal song.
By silent prayer on every pleading tongue
Man finds relief is sweet as faith is strong.

There is no rival to the comfort shared
Within this country church where hearts are bared.

The town is man's world,
but this country life
is of God.
—William Cowper

A country church rises out of a cornfield in Tioga County, Pennsylvania.
Photo by J. Irwin/H. Armstrong Roberts.

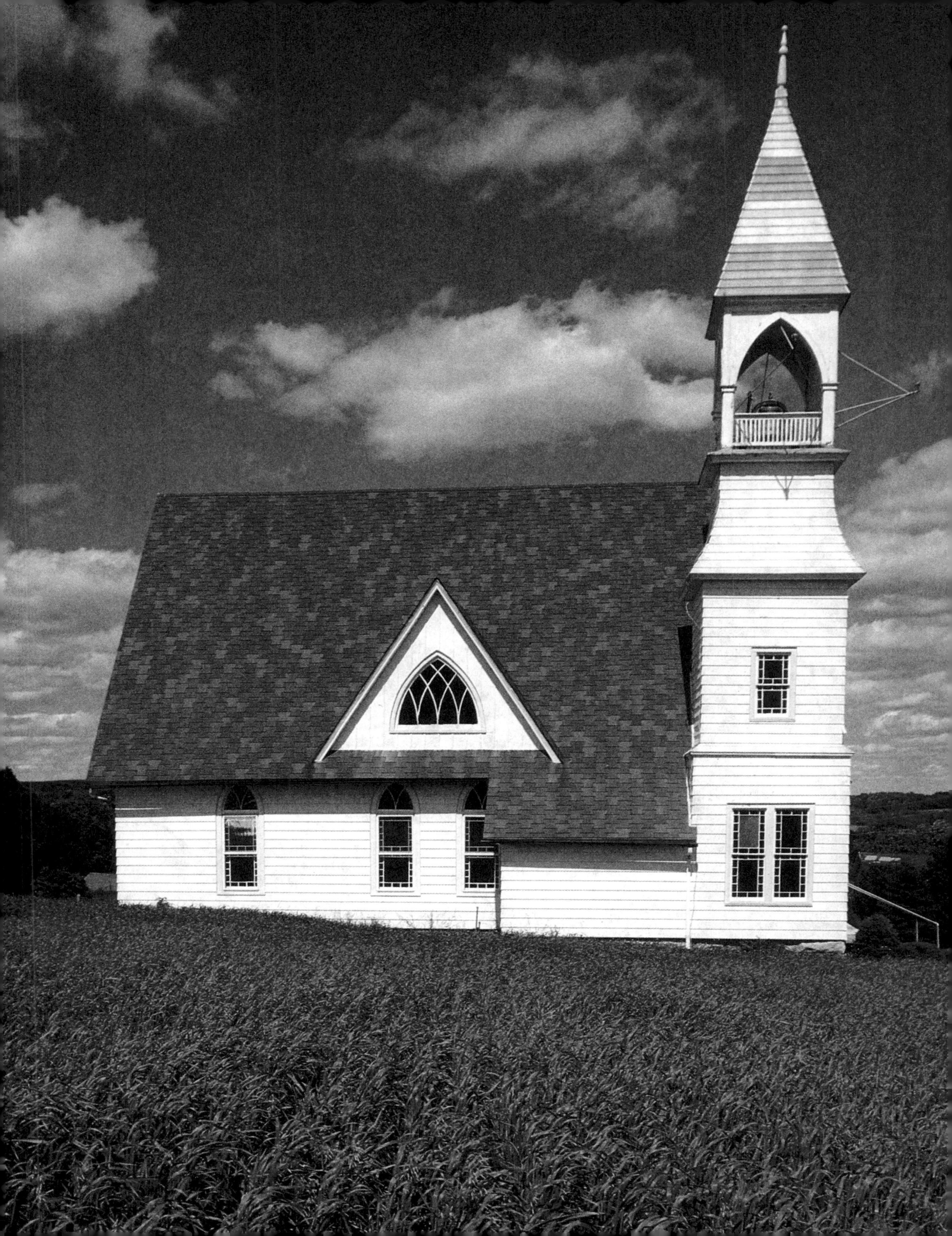

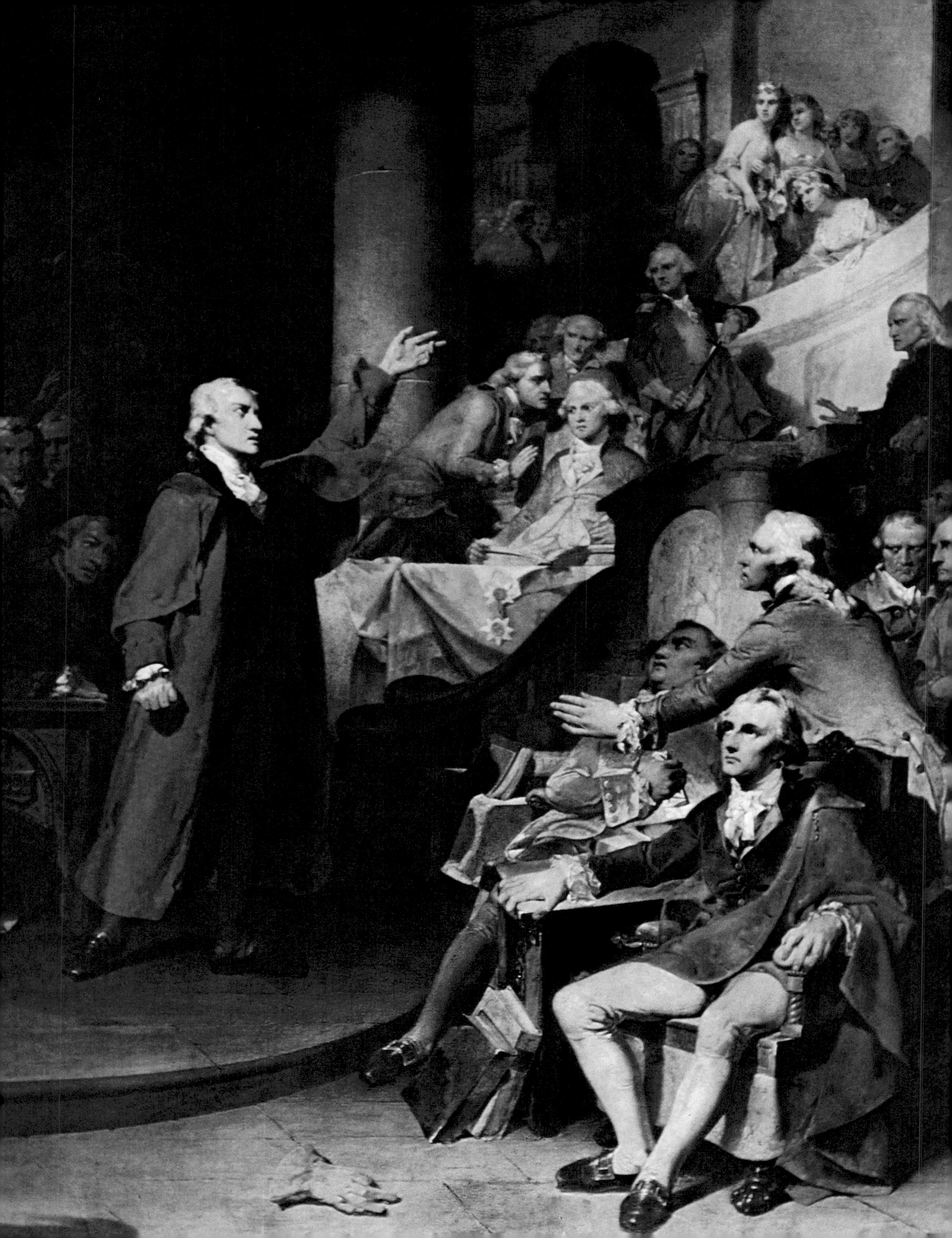

OUR HERITAGE

GIVE ME LIBERTY OR GIVE ME DEATH

Patrick Henry, 1775

I have but one lamp by which my feet are guided; and that is the lamp of experience. I know of no way of judging the future but by the past. And judging by the past, I wish to know what there has been in the conduct of the British ministry for the last ten years, to justify those hopes with which gentlemen have been pleased to solace themselves and the House? Is it that insidious smile with which our petition has lately been received? Trust it not, sir: it will prove a snare to your feet. Suffer not yourselves to be betrayed by a kiss. . . .

Sir, we have done everything that could be done to avert the storm which is now coming on. We have petitioned; we have remonstrated, we have supplicated; we have prostrated ourselves before the throne, and have implored its interposition to arrest the tyrannical hands of the ministry and Parliament. Our petitions have been slighted; our remonstrances have produced additional violence and insult; our supplications have been disregarded; and we have been spurned, with contempt, from the foot of the throne. In vain, after these things, may we indulge the fond hope of peace and reconciliation? There is no longer any room for hope. If we wish to be free—if we mean to preserve inviolate those inestimable privileges for which we have been so long contending—if we mean not basely to abandon the noble struggle in which we have been so long engaged, and which we have pledged ourselves never to abandon until the glorious object of our contest shall be obtained, we must fight! I repeat sir, we must fight! An appeal to arms and to the God of Hosts is all that is left us! . . .

It is vain, sir, to extenuate the matter. Gentlemen may cry, "Peace, Peace!"—but there is no peace. The war is actually begun! The next gale that sweeps from the north will bring to our ears the clash of resounding arms! Our brethren are already in the field! Why stand we here idle? What is it that gentlemen wish? What would they have? Is life so dear, or peace so sweet, as to be purchased at the price of chains and slavery? Forbid it, Almighty God! I know not what course others may take; but as for me, give me liberty, or give me death!

ABOUT THE TEXT

In March of 1775, tension between Great Britain and the American colonies had reached a crisis point. Patrick Henry, a thirty-eight-year-old Virginia lawyer, was an outspoken proponent of American independence. Speaking before the Virginia Legislature at St. John's Church in Richmond, Henry delivered the powerful speech that made the line "Give me liberty, or give me death" a permanent part of American legend. The result was a surge in patriotism throughout the colonies; and within a month, the war for American independence had begun.

Artist Peter Frederick Rothermel (1817–1895) portrays America's history in PATRICK HENRY ADDRESSING THE HOUSE OF BURGESSES. *Image from Superstock.*

FROM

How We Kept the Day

Will Carleton

The great procession came up the street,
With clatter of hoofs and tramp of feet;
There was General Jones to guide the van,
And Corporal Jinks, his right-hand man;
And each was riding his high horse,
And each had epaulettes, of course;
And each had a sash of the bloodiest red,
And each had a shako on his head;
And each had a sword by his left side,
And each had his mustache newly dyed;
    And that was the way
    We kept the day,
The great, the grand, the glorious day,
That gave us—
    Hurray! Hurray! Hurray!
(With a battle or two, the histories say,)
Our national independence!
The great procession came up the street,
With loud da capo, and brazen repeat;
There was Hans, the leader, a Teuton born,
A sharp who worried the E Flat horn;
And Baritone Jake, and Alto Mike,
Who never played anything twice alike;
And Tenor Tom, of conservative mind,
Who always came out a note behind;
And Dick, whose tuba was seldom dumb,
And Bob, who punished the big bass drum.
And when they stopped a minute to rest,
The martial band discoursed its best;
The ponderous drum and the pointed fife
Proceeded to roll and shriek for life;
And Bonaparte Crossed the Rhine, anon,
And The Girl I Left Behind Me came on;
    And that was the way
    The bands did play
On the loud, high-toned, harmonious day,
That gave us—
    Hurray! Hurray! Hurray!
(With some music of bullets, our sires would say,)
Our glorious independence!

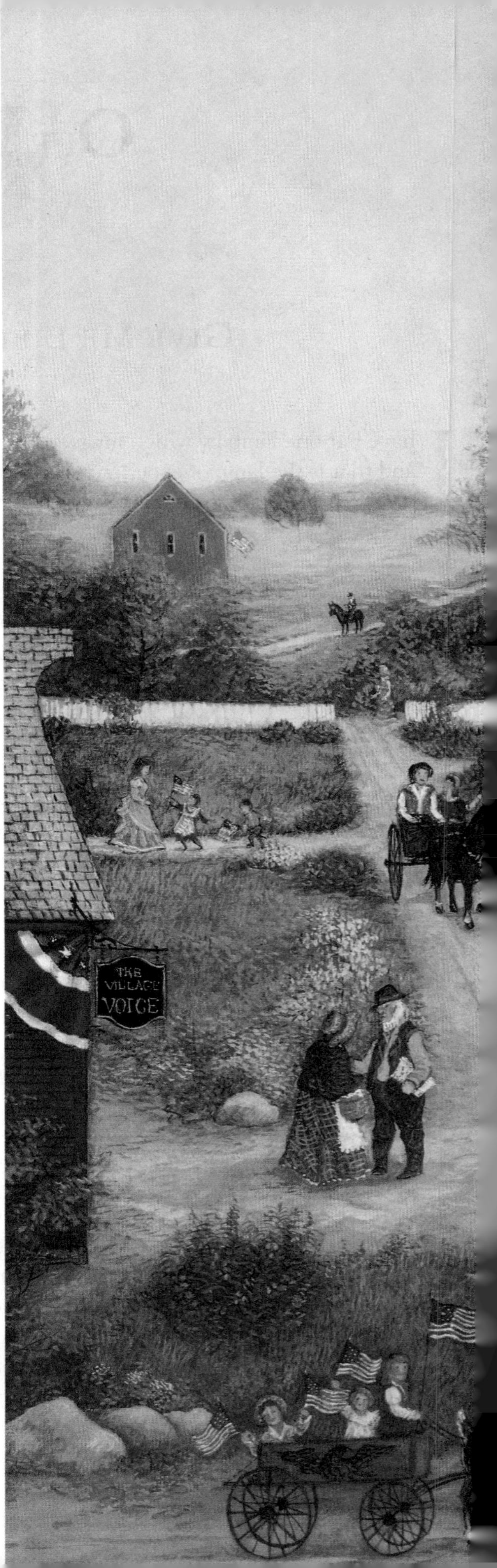
THE VILLAGE VOICE

A small town enjoys the Fourth in the painting FREEDOM CELEBRATION *by artist Linda Nelson Stocks.*

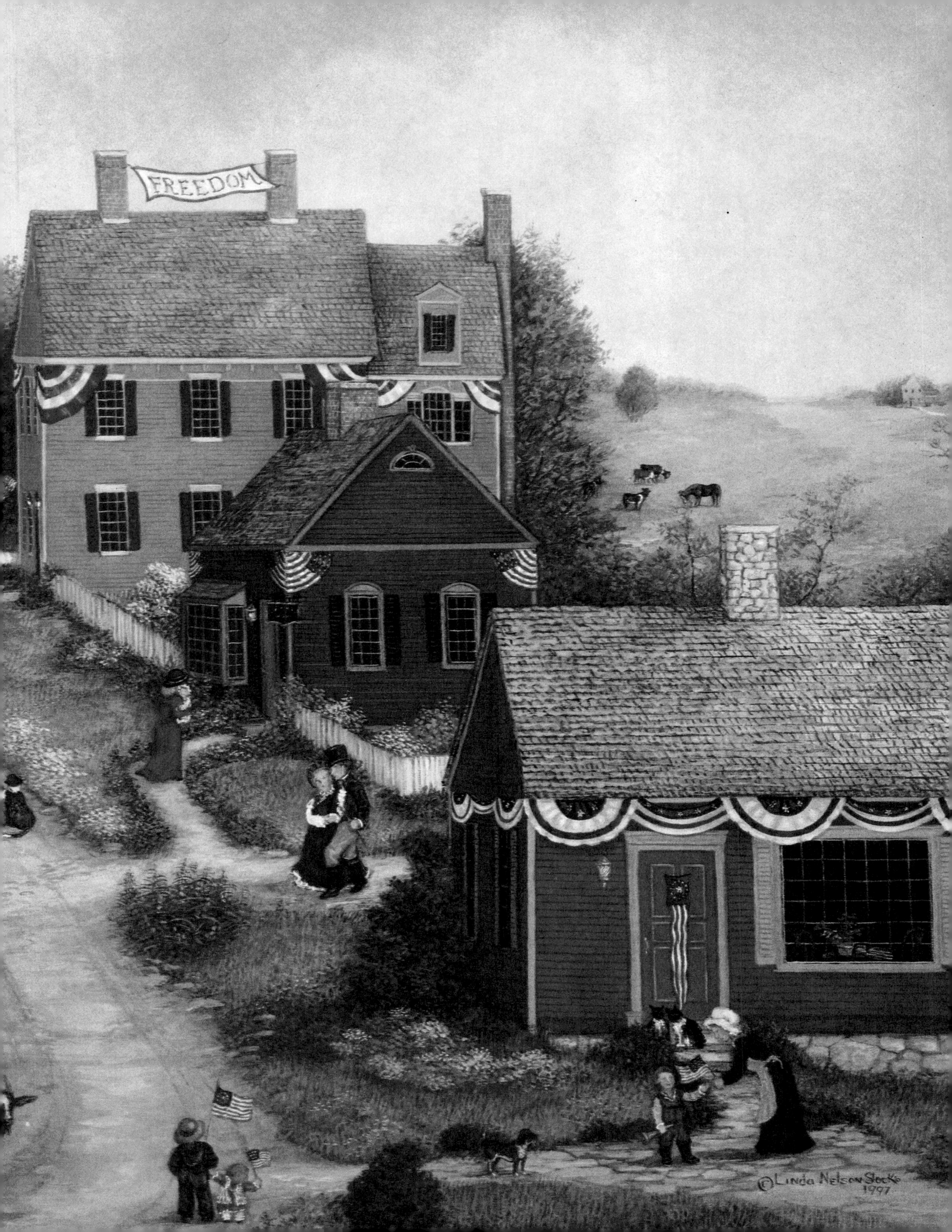
FREEDOM
©Linda Nelson Stocks
1997

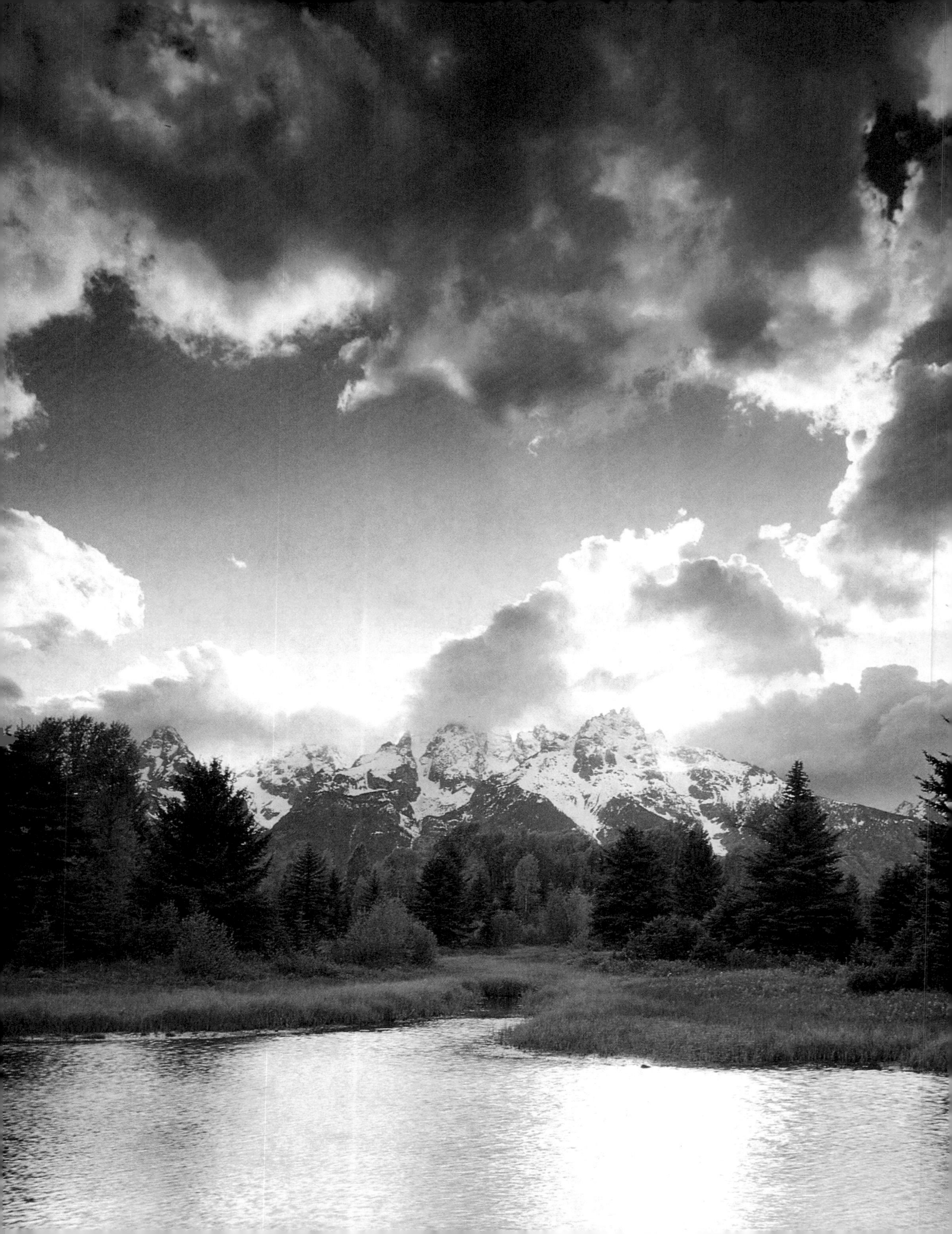

PRAYER FOR THE NATION

Vincent Godfrey Burns

Judge of the nations, hear us;
We rest our faith in Thee.
Stay Thou forever near us
And guide us constantly.
Through all our days protected
By Thy unfailing light,
We shall not be deflected
From paths of truth and right.

Eternal Father, teach us
The courage of the free.
With Thy pure spirit reach us
With faith and charity.
Illumine all around us
With brotherhood and love.
In all our ways surround us
With wisdom from above.

God of the years, remind us
Of our great history,
The memories that bind us
In one fraternity—
Heroes who served before us,
Whose valor paved the way
For this flag floating o'er us—
Oh, bless this land today!

*I think the true discovery of America is
before us. I think the true fulfillment
of our spirit, of our people, of our mighty
and immortal land, is yet to come . . .
certain as the morning, inevitable as noon.*

—Thomas Wolfe

*A sunlit storm cloud hovers over one of America's great treasures,
Wyoming's Teton Mountains. Photo by Dennis Frates/Oregon Scenics.*

Devotions
FROM THE *Heart*

Pamela Kennedy

"For, brethren, ye have been called unto liberty; only use not liberty for an occasion to the flesh, but by love serve one another." Galatians 5:13

USING LIBERTY

My son and I were having a disagreement over the best use of his time on a Saturday afternoon. He had budgeted several hours for skateboarding followed by lunch at a friend's house and an afternoon at the movies. I, on the other hand, suggested he wash the car and spend some time searching for the floor of his room. As we argued the merits of our individual cases, my son ended his presentation with a favorite adolescent refrain: "But, Mom, it's a free country!"

Later, as we wiped down the family van, I considered his assumption. Yes, it is a free country in many respects, but is that freedom liberty to exercise unrestrained selfishness? Does it imply I am free to "do my own thing" and disregard others? Is my liberty a license to ignore obligation and responsibility? I thought how much we'd all suffer if that were the true meaning of freedom. After all, how many of us go to work, keep house, care for our families, or help the needy simply because it suits us?

In the passage from Galatians quoted above, Paul speaks to a people who are new to Christianity. They are not far removed from the restrictive confines of their former religious traditions. He encourages them to enjoy the freedom of spirit offered through their belief in Christ. Like adolescents, however, they employed their newfound independence to bicker among themselves, lord over one another, and ignore the needs of their neighbors. They had become selfish. If these Galatians lived today we might hear them declare: "I've got to look out for number one!" "This is my time for me."

Paul lovingly offers some advice to these spiritual

adolescents, advice that is just as helpful today as it was almost two thousand years ago. The Amplified Bible puts it this way: "Do not let your freedom . . . be an excuse for selfishness, but through love you should serve one another."

Considering this admonition, I am grateful for the men and women who used their freedom to enrich my life. My parents worked hard, but they always made time for church service and volunteer work in the community, and often I was included in these adventures. I had teachers who freely gave of their advice and encouragement to help me grow academically as well as emotionally. When I was grieving or overwhelmed by circumstances, I recall neighbors who spent their free time comforting me and providing practical help to lighten my load. Through the years I have often been the blessed beneficiary of others' liberty. Now I wondered how I could effectively pass along this lesson to my unhappy son.

As we gathered up the wet towels and I emptied the bucket, I watched my son coiling the hose around the water spigot. His shoulders slumped and every movement showed discouragement.

"What time is the movie?" I asked.

"One-thirty," he replied. "But there's no way I can make it now. I still have to clean my room, and it's a half-mile walk to Mark's house."

"How about if I helped you with your room and then drove you and Mark to the movie?"

"Why would you do that?" he challenged.

"Well," I replied with a smile, "like you said, it's a free country."

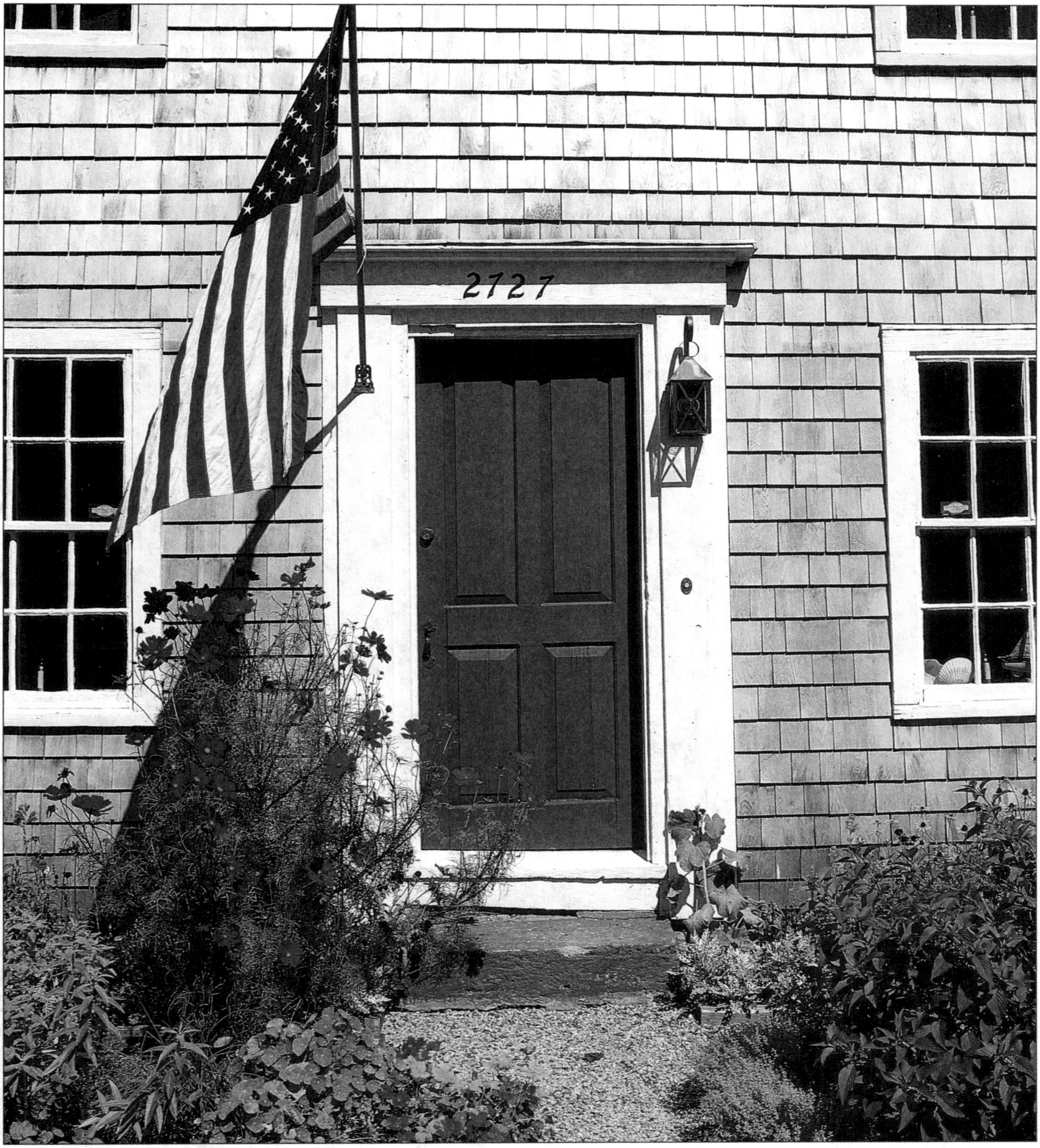
2727

Old Glory welcomes visitors to this historical home in Pennsylvania. Photo by D. Petku/H. Armstrong Roberts.

Prayer: *Dear Father, thank You for the freedom I enjoy. Help me to remember that this liberty is not given so I may indulge myself, but so I may be free to do Your will and serve others. Amen.*

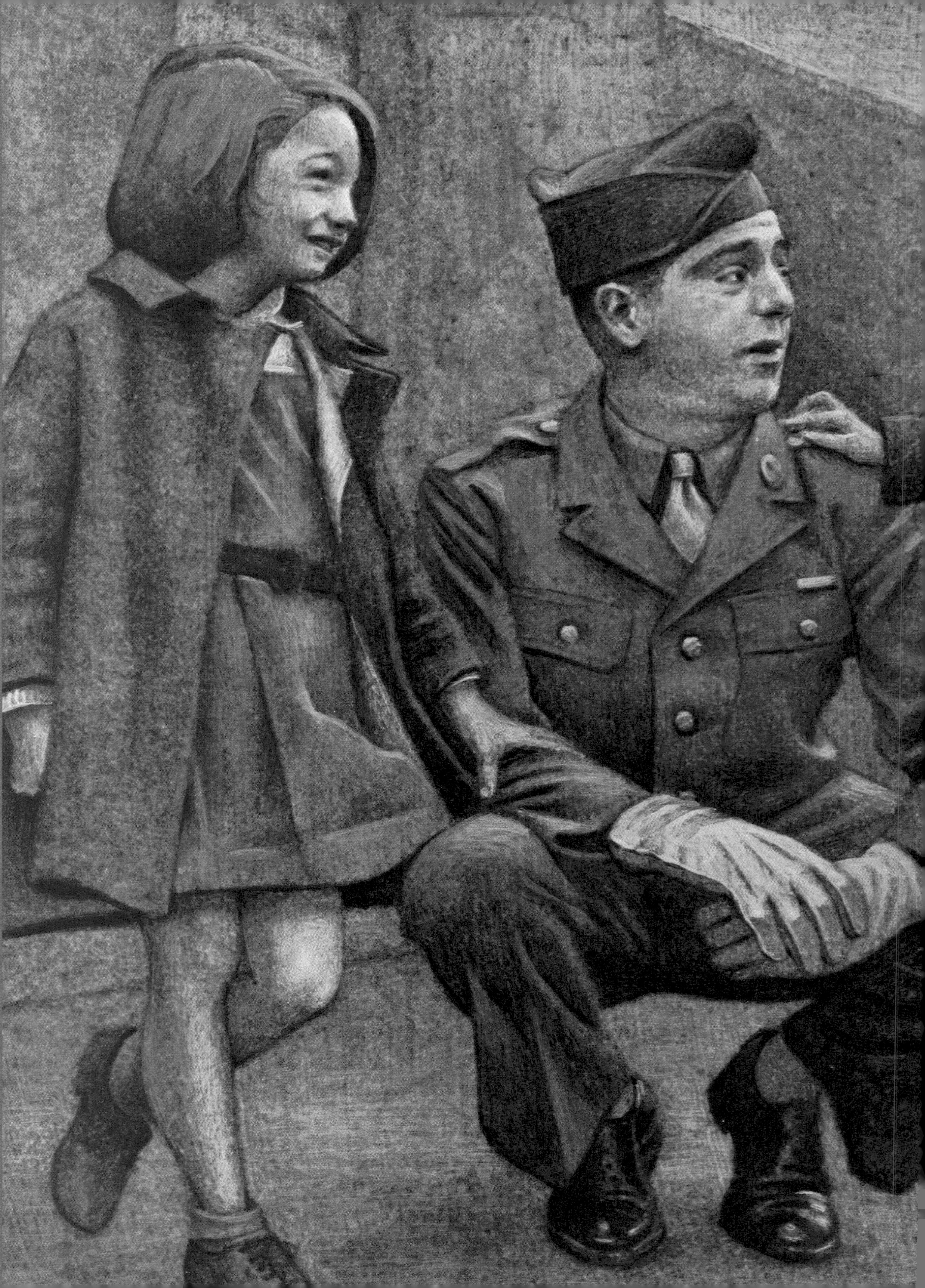

FATHER & THE FOURTH

Grace V. Watkins

Each Independence Day we loved to see
Him loose Old Glory in the morning light
And draw it up until it fluttered high
Within the summer air, sturdy and bright.
"Remember, children," Father used to say,
"We love our country with a heartfelt love;
But we are citizens of another land,
The kingdom of the holy God above."
And always when he spoke the words, his face,
His voice were like a shining, singing prayer.
Although on earth he won no lofty place,
The flags of faith within our hearts are fair
And bright and strong, whatever winds may blow,
Because of what he told us long ago.

Two daughters listen carefully to their father's words in this painting entitled 1940 by artist Martijn Heilig.

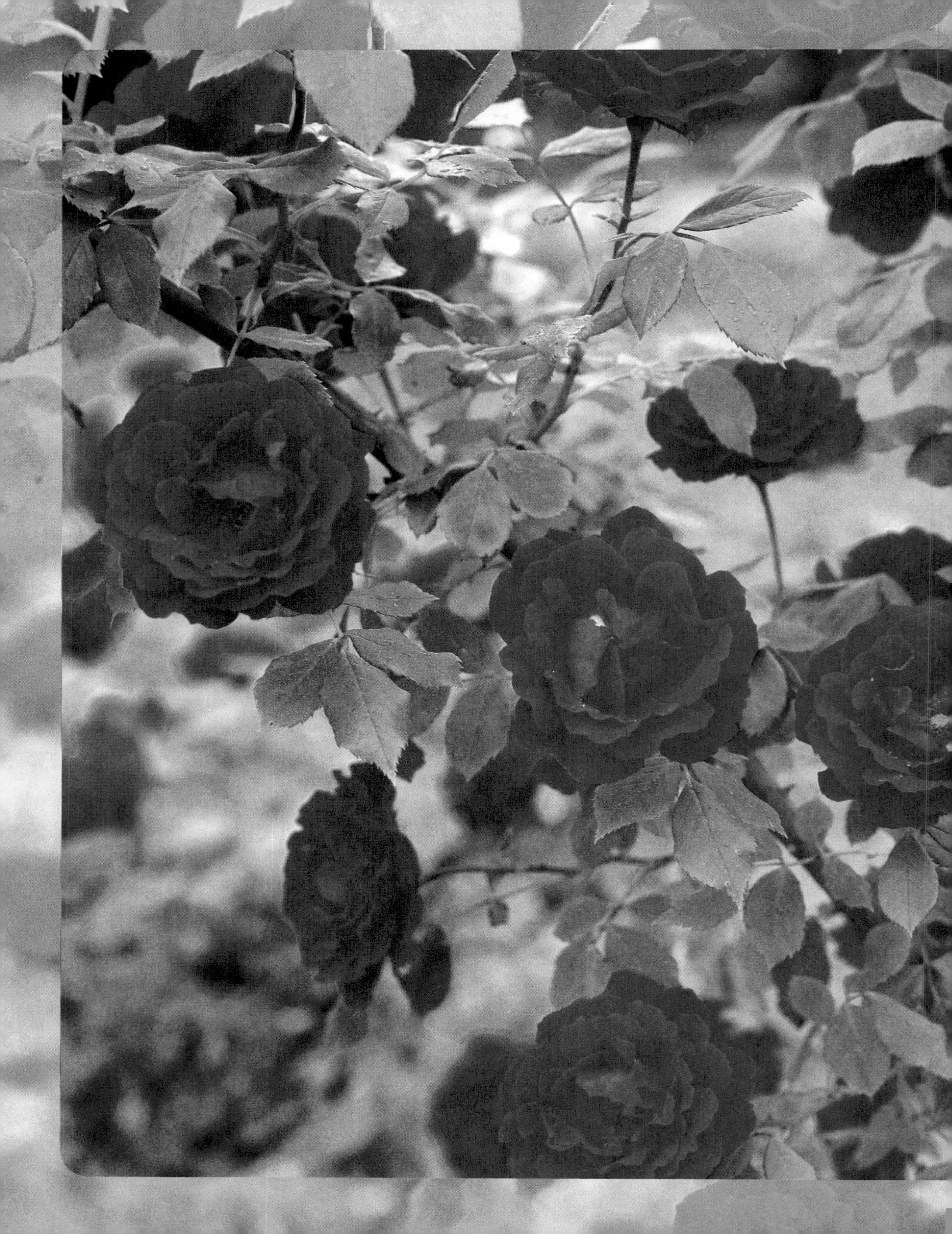

Like a Rose

Evelynn Merilatt Boal

Comes first the bud
    with petals folded tight.
When touched by sun's
    sweet warmth and rays of light,
It opens full,
    becomes a lovely sight.
And that is how
    a special friendship grows.
Warmed by the love
    another person shows,
The tiny bud
    becomes a full-blown rose.

The Rose

Theodore Roethke

And I think of roses, roses,
White and red, in the wide six-hundred-foot greenhouses,
And my father standing astride the cement benches,
Lifting me high over the four-foot stems, the Mrs. Russells,
    and his own elaborate hybrids.
And how those flowerheads seemed to flow toward me,
    to beckon me, only a child, out of myself.

What need for heaven, then,
With that man, and those roses?

Red roses open to the morning sun in Cape Cod, Massachusetts.
Photo by William Johnson/Johnson's Photography.

INDELIBLE LOVE MARKED THE PAGES

Arthur Bowler

I watched intently as my little brother was caught in the act. He sat in the corner of the living room, a pen in one hand and my father's brand new hymnbook in the other.

As my father walked into the room, my brother cowered slightly; he sensed that he had done something wrong. From a distance I could see that he had opened my father's new hymnal and scribbled in it the length and breadth of the first page with a pen.

Now, staring at my father fearfully, he and I both waited for his punishment. And as we waited, there was no way we could have known that our father was about to teach us deep and lasting lessons about life and family, lessons that become even clearer through the years.

My father picked up his prized hymnal, looked at it carefully, and then sat down, without saying a word. Books were precious to him; he was a clergyman and the holder of several degrees. For him, books were knowledge, and yet he loved his children.

What he did next was remarkable. Instead of punishing my brother, instead of scolding or yelling or reprimanding, he sat down, took the pen from my brother's hand, and then wrote in the book himself, alongside the scribbles John had made:

John's work, 1959, age 2. How many times have I looked into your beautiful face and into your warm, alert eyes looking up at me and thanked God for the one who has now scribbled in my new hymnal. You have made the book sacred, as have your brothers and sister to so much of my life.

Wow, I thought. This is punishment?

The years and the books came and went. Our family experienced what all families go through and perhaps a little bit more: triumph and tragedy, prosperity and loss, laughter and tears. We gained grandchildren, we lost a son. We always knew our parents loved us and that one of the proofs of their love was the hymnal by the piano.

From time to time we would open it, look at the scribbles, read my father's expression of love, and feel uplifted. Now I know that through this simple act my father taught us how every event in life has a positive side—if we are prepared to look at it from another angle—and how precious it is when our lives are touched by little hands.

But he also taught us about what really matters in life: people, not objects; tolerance, not judgment; love, not anger. Now I too am a father and, like my dad, a clergyman and holder of degrees. But unlike my father, I do not wait for my daughters to secretly take books from my bookshelf and scribble in them. From time to time I take one down—not just a cheap paperback but a book that I know I will have for many years to come—and I give it to one of my children to scribble or write her name in.

And as I look at my daughters' artwork, I think about my father, the lessons he taught me, and the love he has for us and which I have for my children—love that is at the very heart of a family. I think about these things and I smile. Then I whisper, "Thank you, Dad."

A father and daughter share a book and a memory. Photo by Superstock.

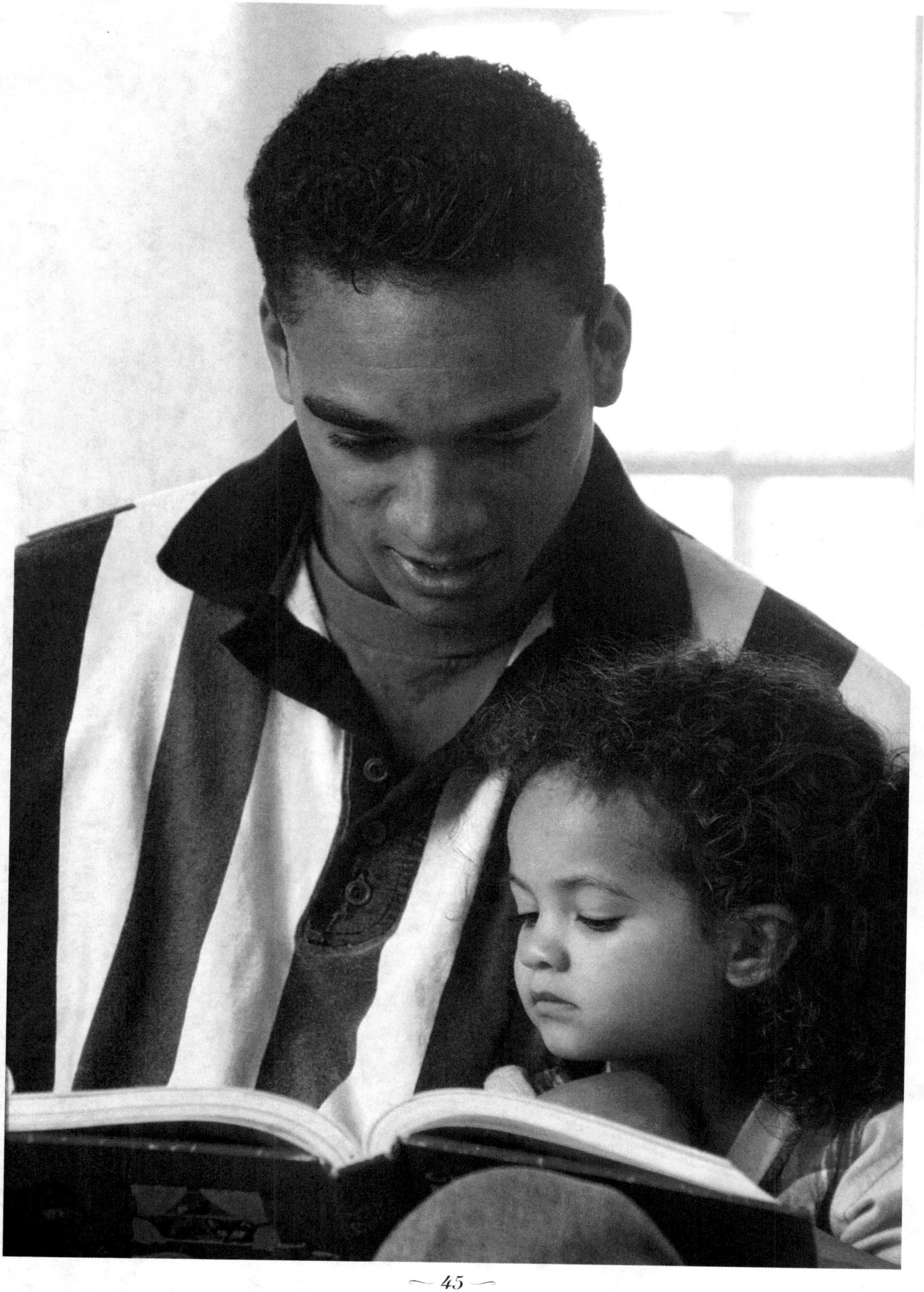

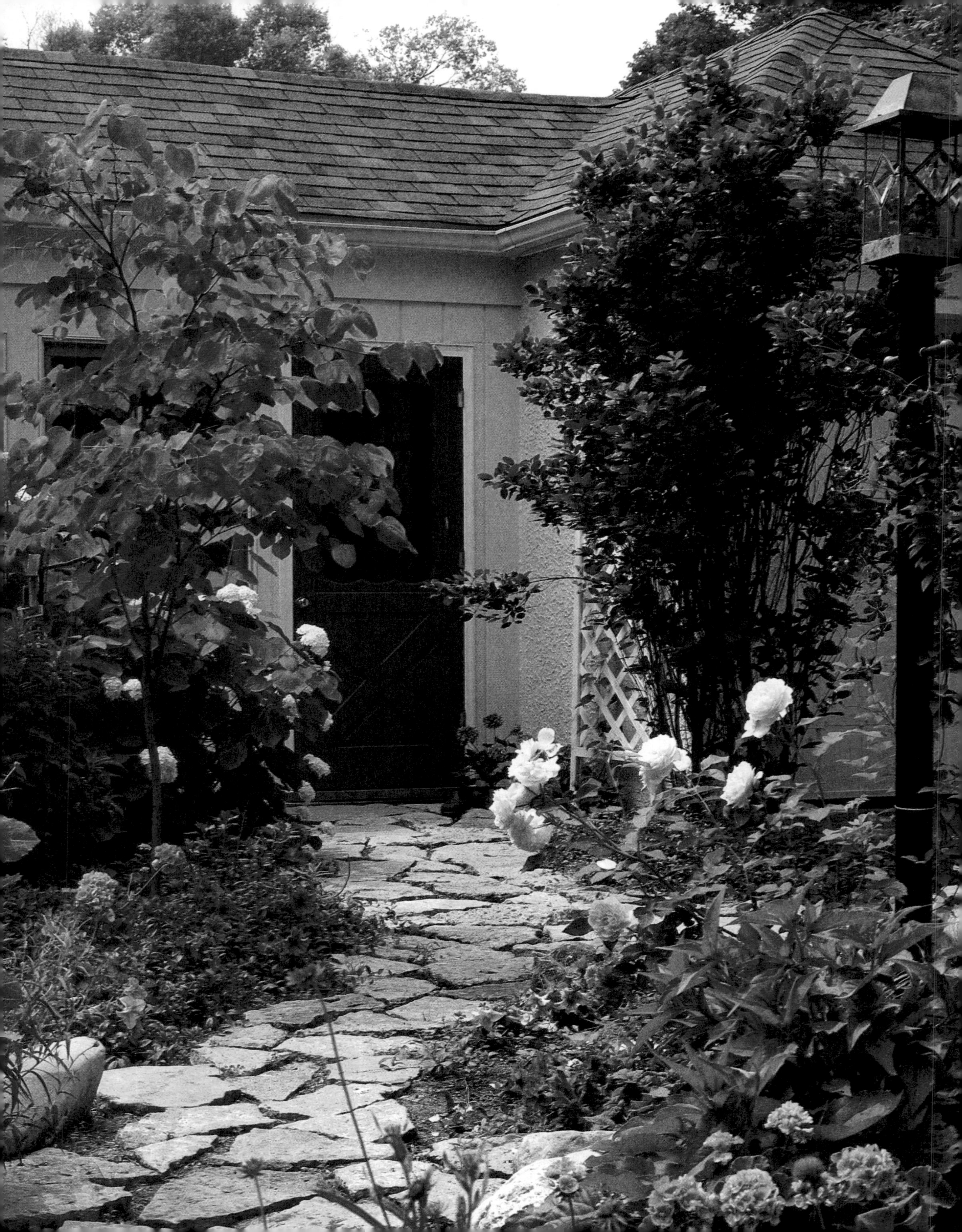

Homecoming

Virginia Blanck Moore

"Your father's coming," she used to say—
And he would be too, a block away.
And I never could figure out how she knew,
Because there she'd be, maybe stirring the stew,
Clear away from the window or any door.
She couldn't have seen him, and what's more,
I'd strain my ears, and I couldn't hear
His step at all. It was certainly queer.

So once I asked, and I heard her say
These words I remember to this very day:
"Some day you'll know, just wait a spell.
When one you love comes, your heart can tell."
And sure enough, I've found it's true.
Both walls and space a heart sees through.
And I can say now with certainty,
"Your daddy's coming!" and there you'll be!

A flagstone path leads the way to a cottage home in Illinois.
Photo by Jessie Walker.

THROUGH MY WINDOW

Pamela Kennedy

Art by Pat Thompson

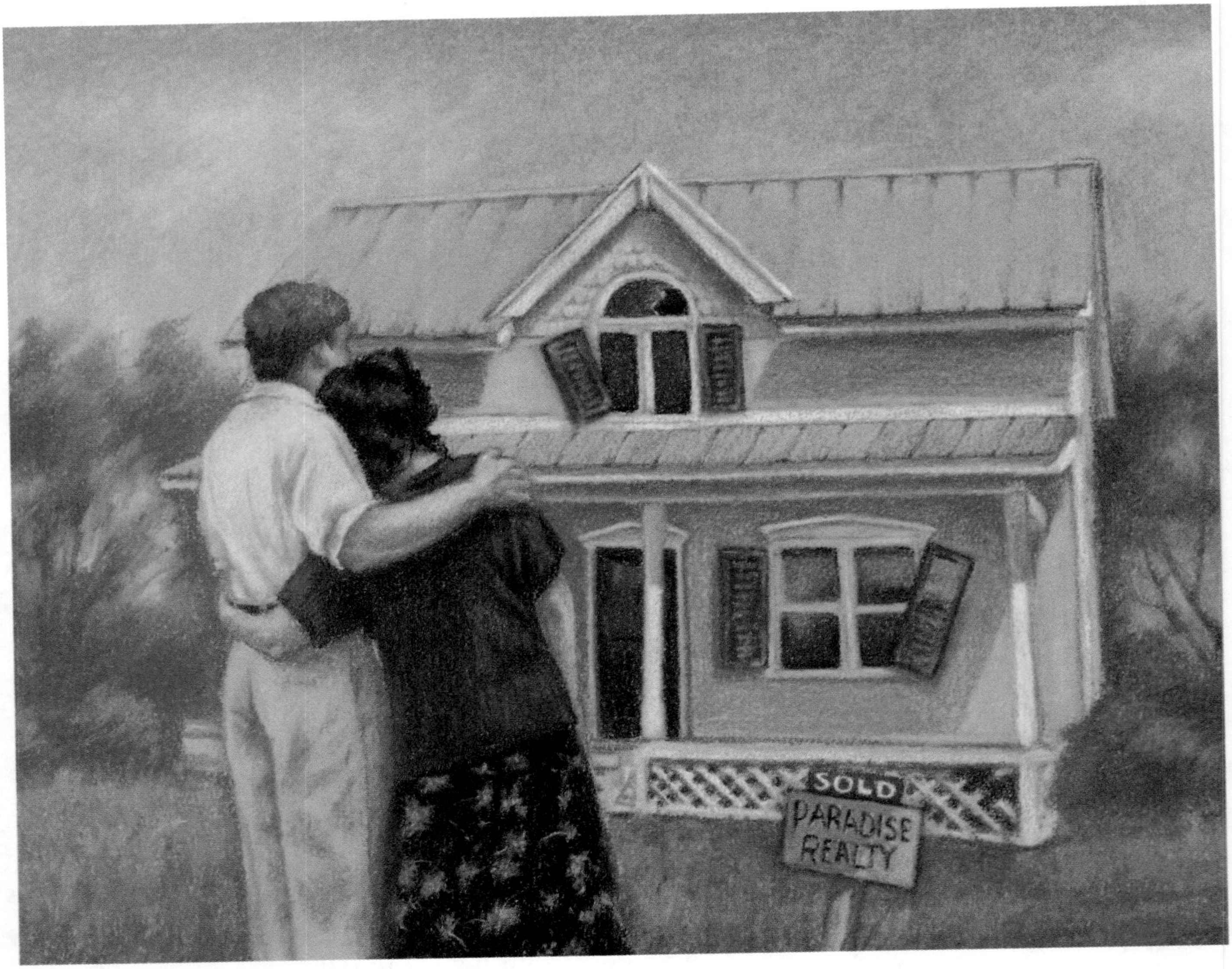
SOLD
PARADISE
REALTY

Adventures in Realtyland

When my husband retired after twenty-eight years in the U.S. Navy, we were ready to settle down. For almost three decades we had moved from coast to coast, living in towns we had never chosen, in houses we had never owned. The number one item on our family agenda was to purchase a home. I couldn't wait to have a place where I didn't need to get permission to change the paint or hang wallpaper, cut down a tree or plant a shrub. As soon as we knew where we wanted to live, we started our adventures in Realtyland.

The first thing we learned is that you need a guide. The guide, commonly referred to as a realtor, negotiates the jungles of Realtyland, conferring with the natives and translating their unique dialect. This is very important, because out in the wilds of the housing market they speak a foreign tongue.

After securing the services of our trusty guide, Valerie, we obtained a copy of the sacred writings titled Multiple Listing Service (MLS) and headed off to bag ourselves a house. Our assumption that the sacred writings provided clear direction was soon dispelled. When the MLS declared, "creative floor plan with panoramic vistas," we discovered what I would describe as a tree house located at the end of a driveway so steep our wheels spun on the dry pavement. "Handyman's haven" meant there were structural problems serious enough to engage several contractors for months. "Ocean view" actually turned out to be a pie-shaped wedge of blue partly visible from the upstairs bathroom window on a clear day. "Breezy living areas" creatively described a house lacking several windows and a large portion of the roof. Adjectives like "nice," "cute," "darling," and "snug" all translate as *tiny* in Realtyland. Phrases such as "great opportunity," "needs TLC," and "priced under market value" are dead giveaways that the place is a dump. When a real estate ad asks you to "use your imagination" as you view a property, you can be sure even Houdini couldn't conjure a way to salvage it. If the decor is described as "cheerful," you can be certain to find wallpaper with teddy bears; and "well loved" almost always means worn out.

Eventually we were able to decipher a bit of the language in this strange land and even converse with some of the less hostile natives. And with Valerie's diligence and skill we finally found a house that met our needs. This did not mean, however, that our work was finished. Now came the even more daunting task of making the deal.

Purchasing in Realtyland is not like going to the store. This is because the prices on houses bear little relationship to what one actually pays. It's sort of like international politics where ambassadors from two hostile nations negotiate a peace agreement that leaves both countries feeling equally frustrated.

In the end each country has a vague feeling of loss and nagging doubts about having received the worst end of the deal.

At this point in our adventure, we were required to participate in a mysterious ritual called escrow. This ritual takes place at a Realtyland shrine: the escrow company. Foreigners are not allowed to actually watch, but as far as I can ascertain, what happens is this: money goes into escrow, and special wizards are paid to pronounce mystical incantations over it. After these ceremonies, the money is distributed to various citizens of Realtyland. I suspect the chief wizard, or escrow agent, is in cahoots with the rulers of Realtyland because you can't get a house there unless you pay him to bless your money.

If your real estate agent is courageous enough to face down the angry sellers and bluffing agents inhabiting the jungles of Realtyland and wise enough to placate the chief wizards of escrow, you may end up as we did, the proud owners of a new home. You will have survived one of the most dangerous and intimidating adventures of the twentieth century. But the adventure is not quite over.

It is important to know that those who successfully return from Realtyland often suffer frequent flashbacks. These are characterized by feelings of panic usually occurring at the beginning of the month when the mortgage payment is due. Often there is also a heightened auditory phenomenon causing one to hear termites and carpenter ants gnawing on the support beams under the house. In addition, a sinking sensation has been known to disturb recent homebuyers when the Federal Reserve announces a drop in interest rates. But I have it on good authority that these symptoms gradually disappear and that the best way to hasten their departure is to hang a sign on your front door declaring "Home Sweet Home."

Pamela Kennedy is a freelance writer of short stories, articles, essays, and children's books. Wife of a retired naval officer and mother of three children, she has made her home on both U.S. coasts and currently resides in Honolulu, Hawaii.

WHAT DAD KNEW

Agnes M. Sloane

He knew the name of every tree that grew
On homeland hills and by the river bend.
When shy and hidden mayflowers bloomed, he knew
Just where to find them; but he'd then pretend
That small folks on these woodsy expeditions
Had found the fragrant flowers all alone.
He welcomed each wildflower by its name,
The blossoms lost when held in his huge hand.
He loved each furry creature, wild or tame,
And reverenced their Maker and His plan.
The outdoors called him under all conditions,
And growing things he treasured as his own.

He knew the birds and where they built their nests;
He knew and told us how they fed their young.
He loved each season, loved the summer best.
He knew the old songs, loved to hear them sung.
He held the key to childhood, safe and warm,
Was happiest when little folks were near.
He knew just what to do to cure a sting;
His mighty hands could gently do their part
To tend to small, bruised fingers. He could bring
Quick comfort to a childish broken heart.
His mighty arms a bulwark from all harm;
His life, if need be, fortress from all fear.

He knew the streams to fish, could always find
A safe place where young fishermen could stay.
He'd bait their hooks, untangle twisted lines,
Then let them fish the happy hours away.
He'd scorn the whiners and the winners praise
And say 'twas fun to have the kids along!
He knew the ways of love. No ancient knight
Could be more gallant to his lady fair.
He'd proffer wildflowers, berries red and bright,
Wild cherries, or some fern of maidenhair.
And Mom, accepting with a queenly grace,
Caressed the gift and hummed a happy song.

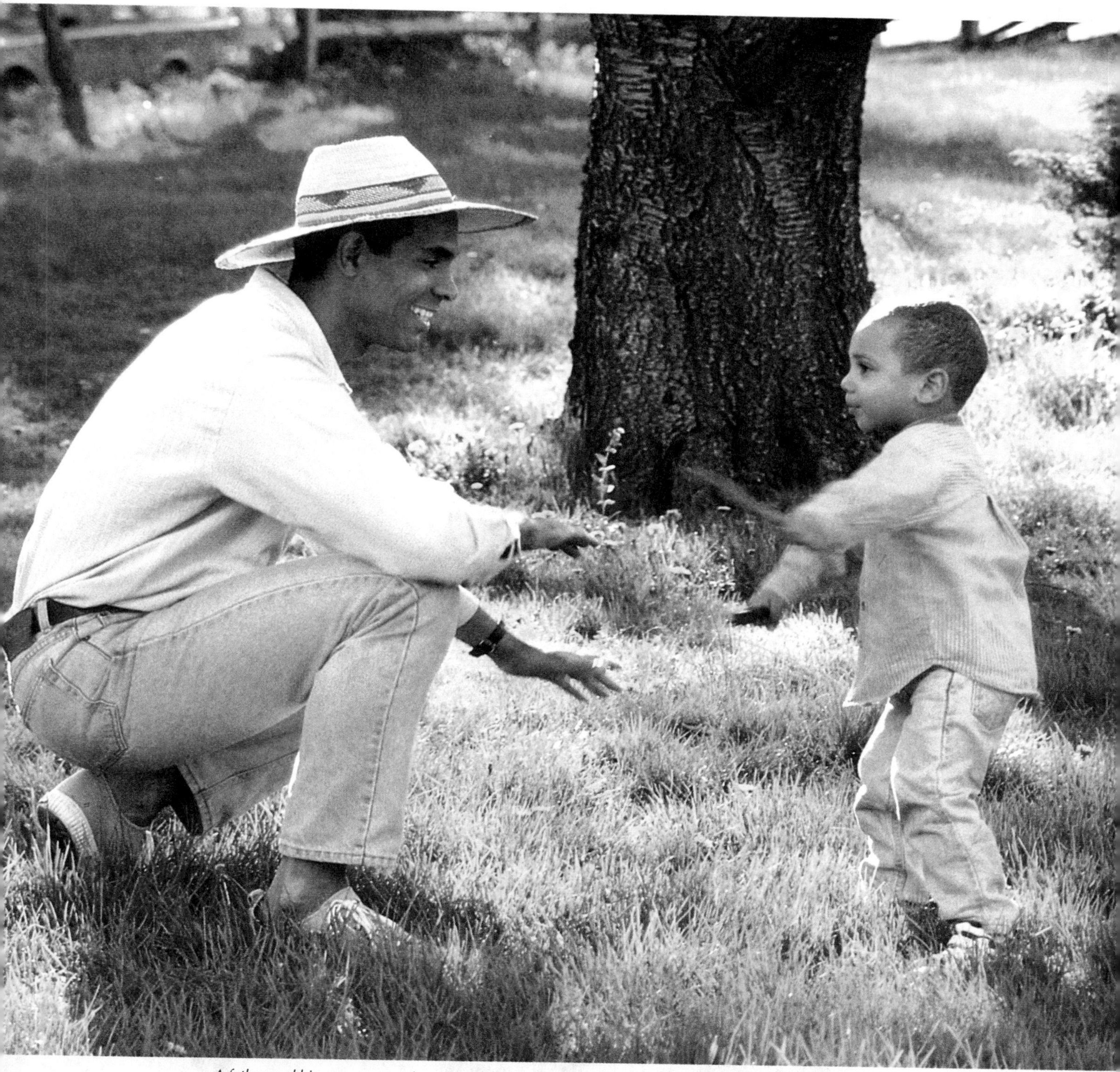

A father and his young son enjoy a warm day in the park. Photo by Lindy Powers/International Stock.

He viewed the distant peaks as feudal kings
Surveyed their captured lands in ancient days;
For hills and lakes were his. All living things
Were miracles to love and offer praise.
Unorthodox, perhaps, to standard view
His way of worship of his God above!

He scorned the city ways and city streets;
He liked to call his neighbors by their names
And liked to feel the earth beneath his feet.
He had no thoughts of wealth nor worldly praise.
A lifetime could not teach me what he knew!
I think he learned it in the school of love.

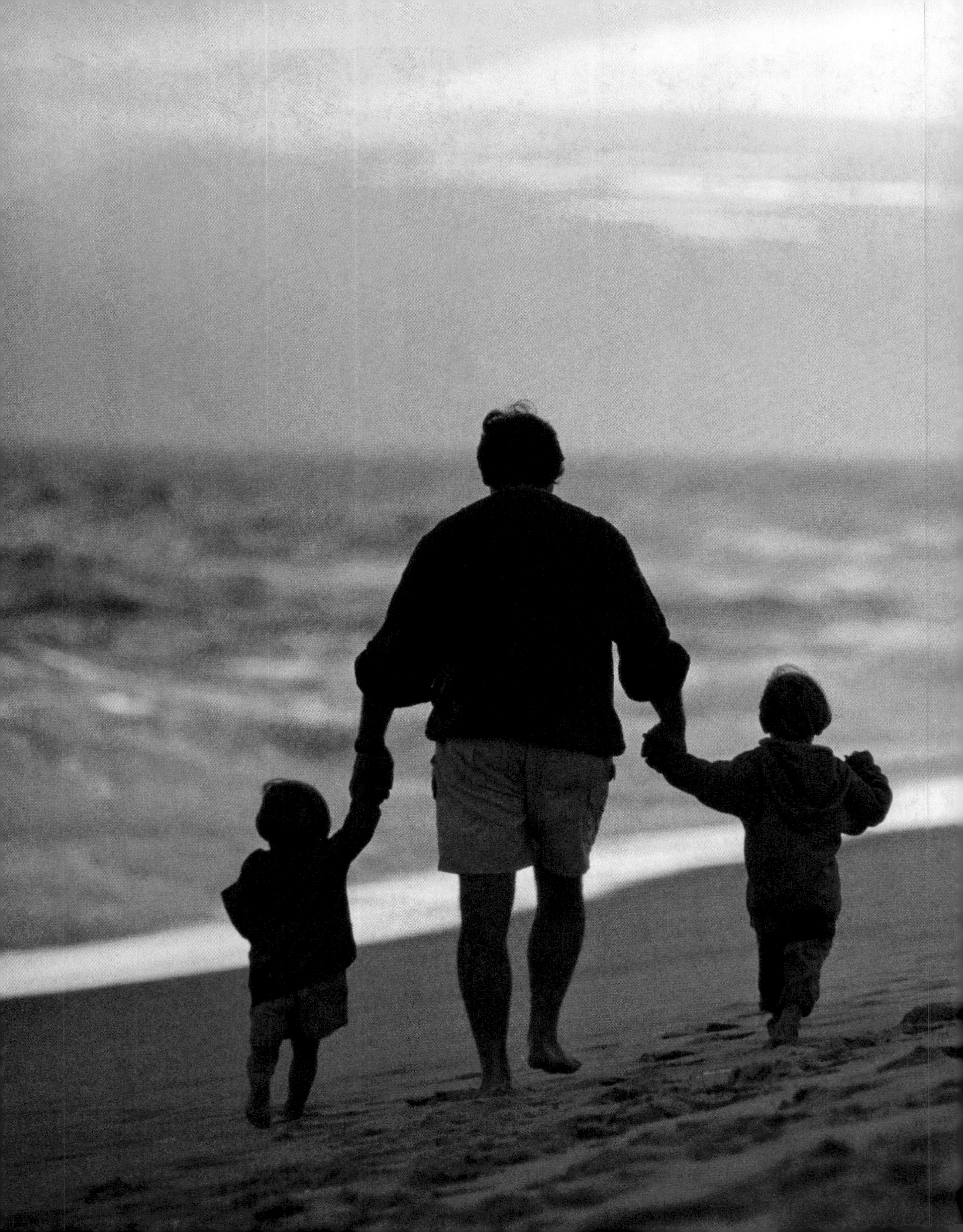

THE SECRET HEART

Robert P. Tristram Coffin

Across the years he could recall
His father one way best of all.

In the stillest hour of night
The boy awakened to a light.

Half in dreams, he saw his sire
With his great hands full of fire.

The man had struck a match to see
If his son slept peacefully.

He held his palms each side the spark
His love had kindled in the dark.

His two hands were curved apart
In the semblance of a heart.

He wore, it seemed to his small son,
A bare heart on his hidden one,

A heart that gave out such a glow
No son awake could bear to know.

It showed a look upon a face
Too tender for the day to trace.

One instant, it lit all about,
And then the secret heart went out.

But it shone long enough for one
To know that hands held up the sun.

A day of sand and sun ends with a quiet family walk.
Photo by Barbara Peacock/FPG International.

A SLICE OF LIFE

Edgar A. Guest

AT SUGAR CAMP

At Sugar Camp the cook is kind
And laughs the laugh we knew as boys;
And there we slip away and find
Awaiting us the old-time joys.
The catbird calls the selfsame way
She used to in the long ago,
And there's a chorus all the day
Of songsters it is good to know.

The killdeer in the distance cries;
The thrasher, in her garb of brown,
From tree to tree in gladness flies.
Forgotten is the world's renown,
Forgotten are the years we've known;
At Sugar Camp there are no men;
We've ceased to strive for things to own;
We're in the woods as boys again.

Our pride is in the strength of trees,
Our pomp the pomp of living things;
Our ears are tuned to melodies
That every feathered songster sings.
At Sugar Camp our noonday meal
Is eaten in the open air,
Where through the leaves the sunbeams steal
And simple is our bill of fare.

At Sugar Camp in peace we dwell
And none is boastful of himself;
None plots to gain with shot and shell
His neighbor's bit of land or pelf.
The roar of cannon isn't heard,
There stilled is money's tempting voice;
Someone detects a new-come bird
And at her presence all rejoice.

At Sugar Camp the cook is kind;
His steak is broiling o'er the coals
And in its sputtering we find
Sweet harmony for tired souls.
There, sheltered by the friendly trees,
As boys we sit to eat our meal,
And, brothers to the birds and bees,
We hold communion with the real.

Edgar A. Guest began his illustrious career in 1895 at the age of fourteen when his work first appeared in the Detroit Free Press. *His column was syndicated in over three hundred newspapers, and he became known as "The Poet of the People."*

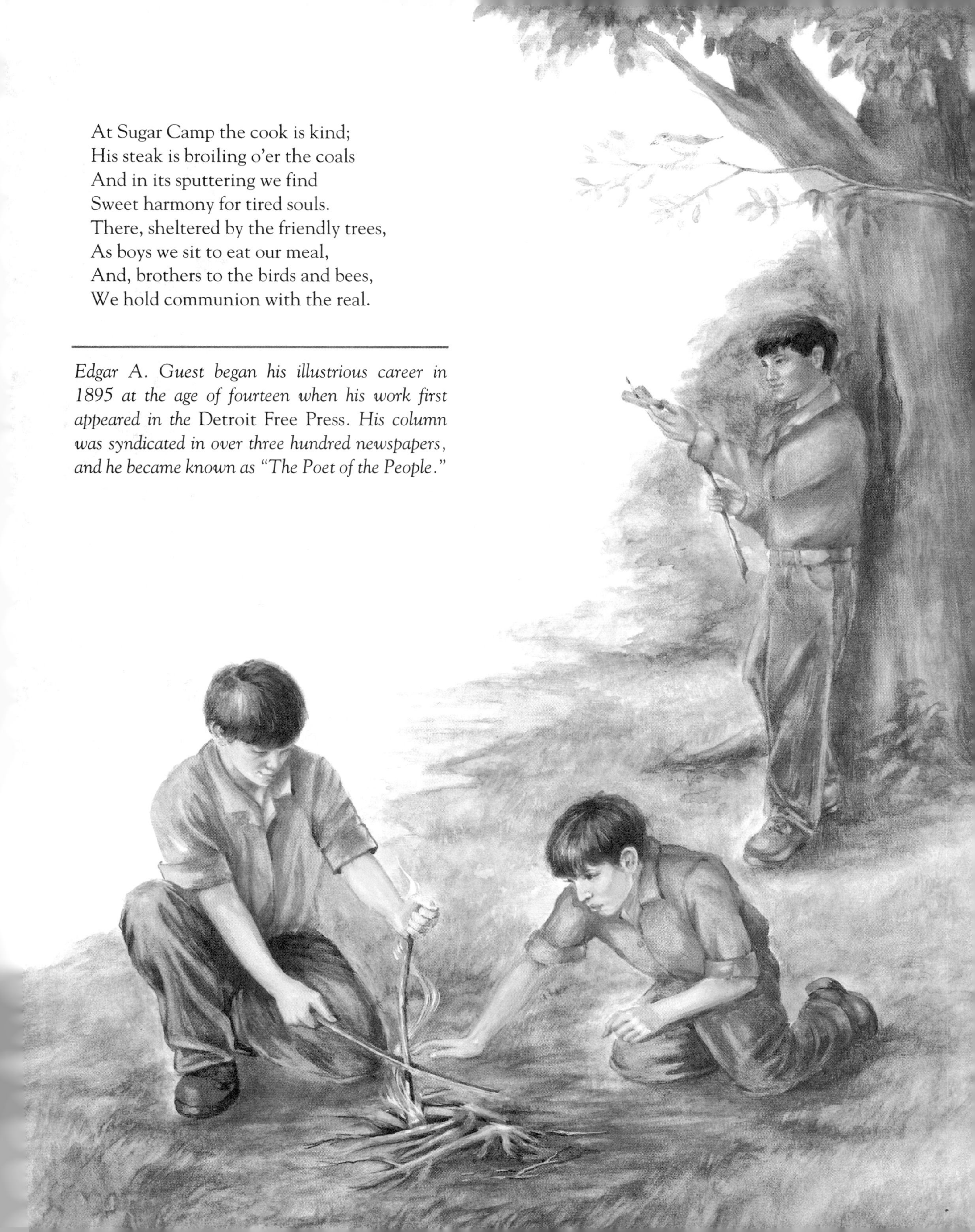

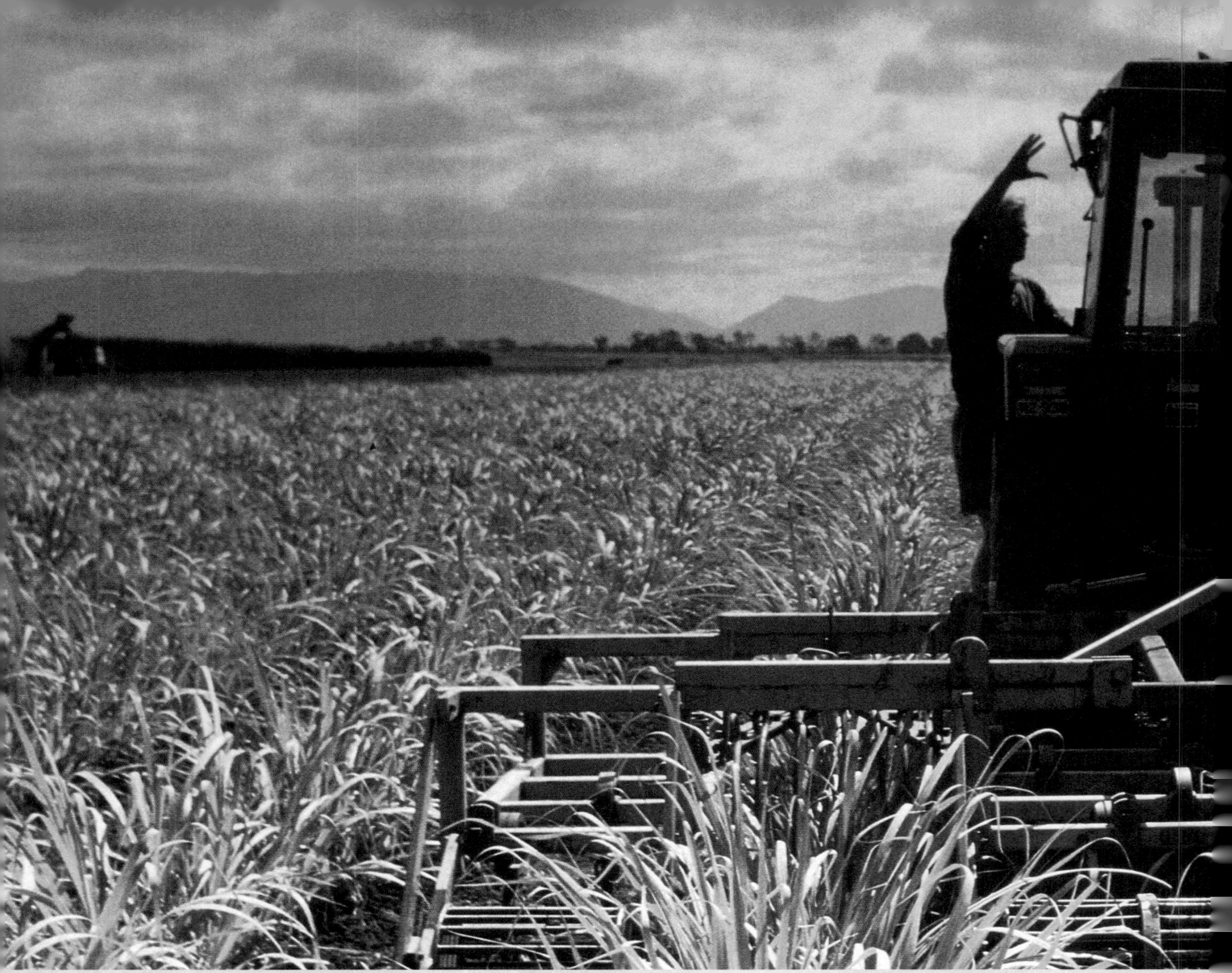

My Father Was a Farmer

S. Omar Barker

My father was a farmer,
A strong, good man;
Straight were the rows
Where his sharp plow ran.

Straight were the thoughts
In his unschooled head,
And straight out of Scripture
The life he led.

Gnarled were his fingers
From life-long toil,
But mellow his heart
That loved the soil.

Close after God
In his soul came labor,
And an equal feeling
For every neighbor.

My father was a farmer
Who knew the worth
Of kinship with
The planted earth.

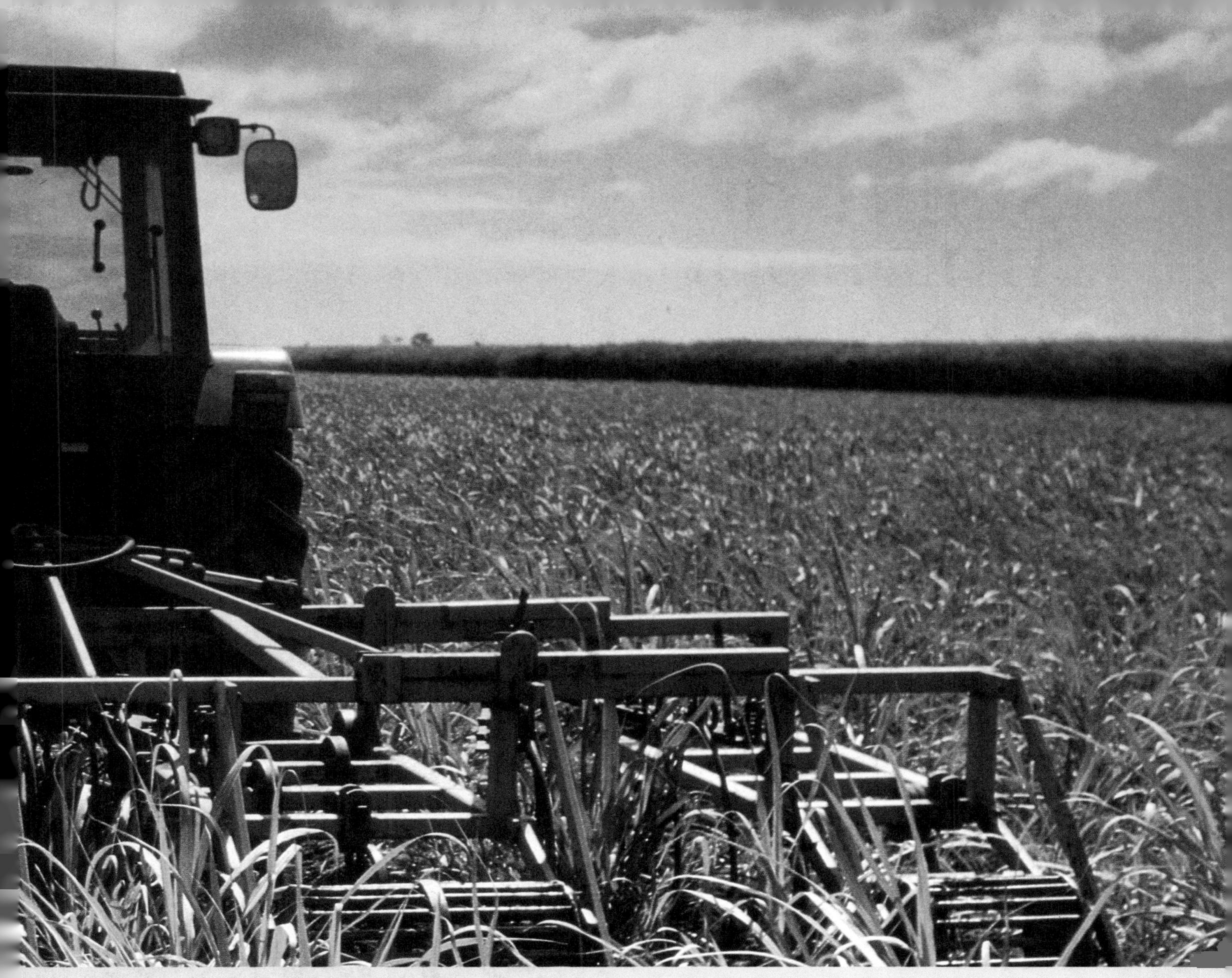

Heritage

Martha D. Tourison

Land is my heritage.
Acres that leap boulders and mountains,
Cascading their waters into churning
pools below.
Valleys checker-boarded with
woodland patches and yellow wheat.
Walls of stone encircling sheep.
Life is good to me and mine.

Harvest sheaved and gathered—
dappled mare and I trot home.
Smoke spirals from my chimneys
Framed against a crimson sky.
Sire to sire and now to me.

Will the son that watches yonder
Love this land as I?

A farmer surveys his fields of sugarcane in Australia. Photo by Frank Grant/International Stock.

SCENT OF CHILDHOOD

Jane Merchant

Dad was the scent of hayfields in the sun.
The faintest drifting fragrances of clover
Undo for me all that the years have done.
While they remain, my childhood
    is not over.
Dad is beside me, brown as earth, and good
As clear, cool water on a thirsty day,
And all I have experienced and withstood
Is gone, at any whiff of new-mown hay.
And Mother was the smell
    of new bread, browned
To crusty, crisp perfection. There may be
Some folk whose childhood, lost,
    is never found,
But mine remains immediate to me,
For always all the years between have fled
At scent of new-mown hay,
    of new-made bread.

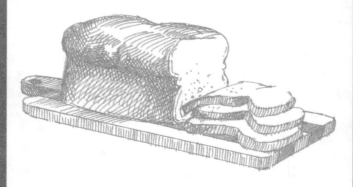

Alaska's Chugach Mountains overlook a field of freshly rolled hay.
Photo by Jeff Gnass.

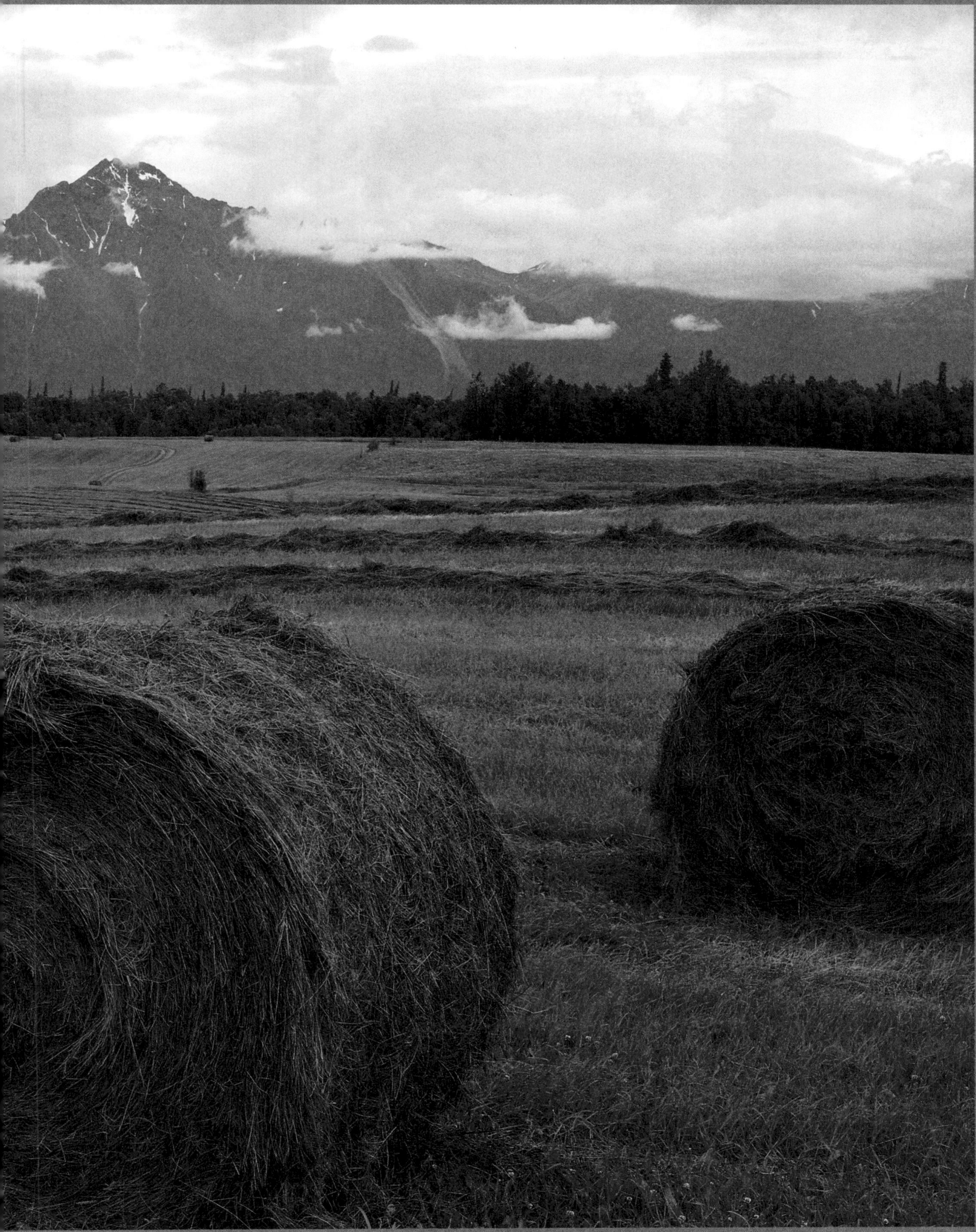

Pear Tree

Gertrude Ryder Bennett

Grandfather stood
Beneath this tree.
I was no higher
Than his knee.
He picked a pear
And gave it to me.

Like flash of light
I can recall
I stood near his chair
And that is all;
The rest is hidden
Beyond time's wall.

His chair remains,
An antique now;
His pears are sweet
As a lover's vow.
In my apron I gather them.
Heavy each bough.

Who is there
To understand
The pattern of life,
Why nature planned
To let the root
Outlive the hand?

A perfect pair of pears waits to be picked. Photo by Superstock.

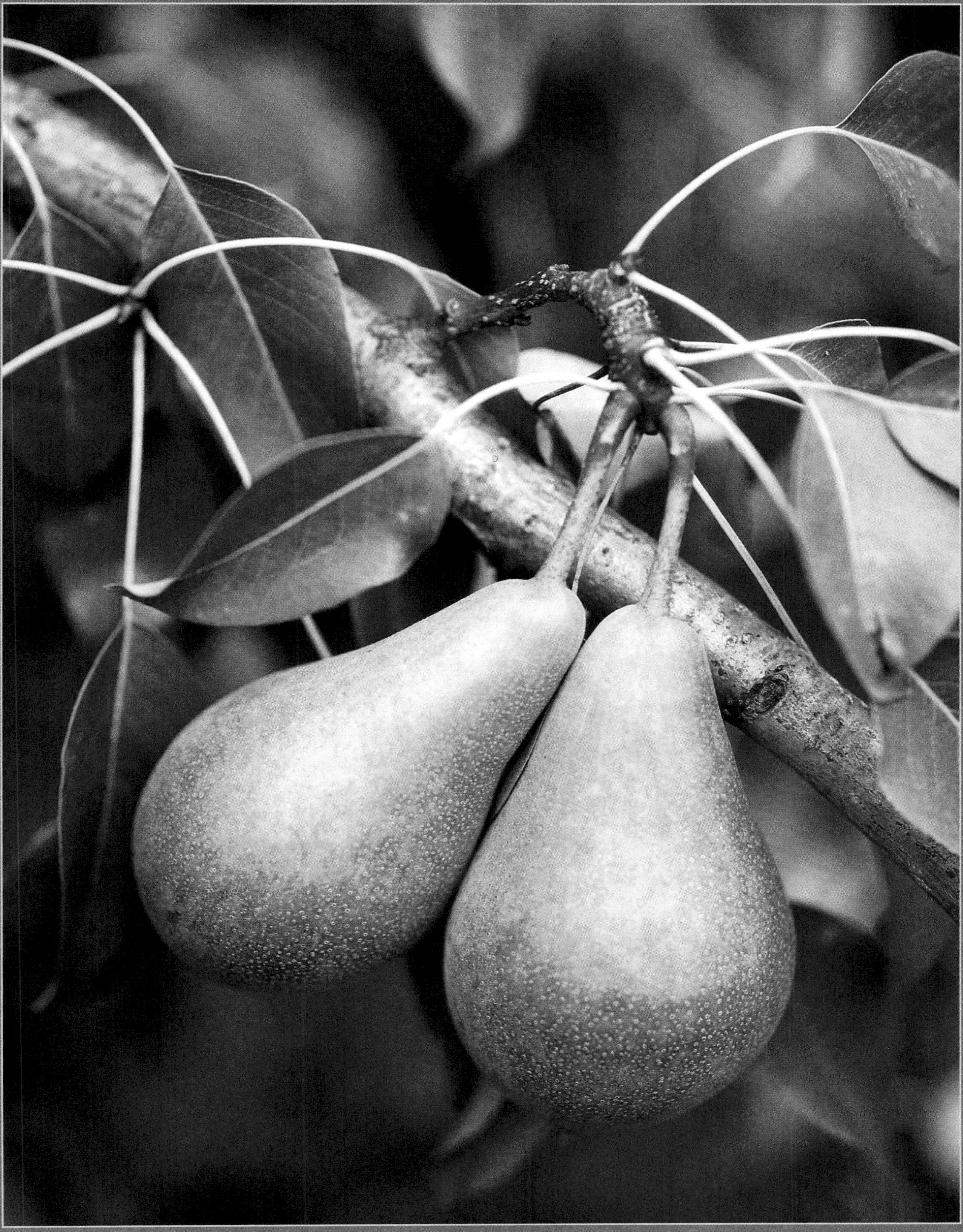

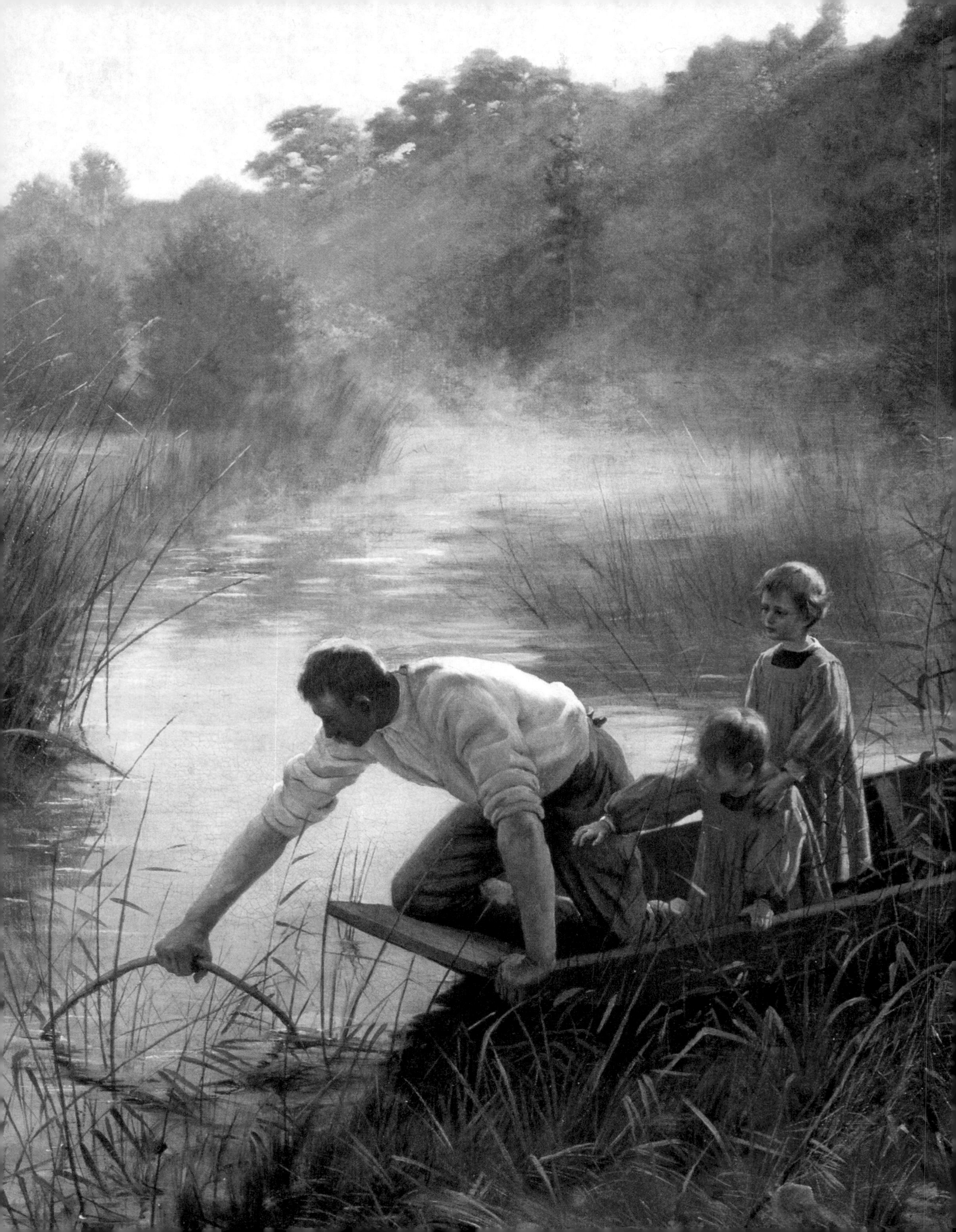

Fishing Time

Grace Shattuck Bail

Out on the blue lake where anglers liked to go,
The emerald dragonflies were flitting low;
And father sometimes paused, took time to wish
That he could leave his shop to catch a fish.

The lake was only five short miles away,
Such humid days, dull trading anyway.
Maybe, he thought, it was good to leave his work
To angle in the lake where bluegills lurk.

Ham sandwiches and deviled eggs he'd take.
So good to eat when he had crossed the lake
On summer days when dragonflies would light
Like jewels against the bonnie boat so white.

I'm glad my father fished some summer days
And found his happiness in simple ways;
I'm also glad he never thought it wrong
To take a little fishing girl along.

In daydreams on the turquoise lake I float
Close to my father in our willing boat;
Although the years are long I sometimes wish
That father still could help me catch a fish.

Two girls watch intently as their father works in THE FISHERMAN'S FAMILY *by
artist Pierre Andre Brouillet (1857–1914). Image from Christie's Images.*

HANDMADE HEIRLOOM

The quilt "Oh, My Papa!" was created by Ami Simms in honor of her father. Images from the book CREATING SCRAPBOOK QUILTS, published by Mallery Press in Flint, Michigan.

SCRAPBOOK QUILT

Michelle Prater Burke

Quilts have long been a forum for remembering. Each scrap of fabric represents a memory of lost times—a toddler's blanket, a first-day-of-school dress, a mother's wedding gown. But memories that weren't made of fabric couldn't be stitched into the quilt, until now. In the book *Creating Scrapbook Quilts*, author Ami Simms shares her passion for scrapbook quilts that can hold every facet of a memory, from black-and-white photographs to war medals. These unique quilts are perfect to commemorate a wedding or anniversary, to honor a beloved relative, or to preserve the memories from a favorite vacation. With Simms's methods, even a novice quilter can incorporate the unique visual images of a scrapbook into quilt form and create a truly unique heirloom.

The main distinction between scrapbook quilts and their predecessors is that the predominant elements in scrapbook quilts are photographs and other images that have been transferred onto fabric. They are also created without a master pattern and therefore require more intuition and imagination (along with a fondness for jigsaw puzzles!).

Scrapbook quilts aren't difficult to construct. The process begins with collecting photographs and other flat items to include in the design. Possibilities range from old letters and children's artwork to ticket stubs and pressed flowers. The book outlines several do-it-yourself methods for transferring the images to fabric; one of the easiest uses transfer paper. Or images can be transferred professionally.

You can then embellish your transferred images to add color, texture, and whimsy to your quilt. Embroidered flowers can be stitched atop a photograph of Grandma among her roses, or real buttons can be sewn onto the snapshot of little Susie in her cardigan. The added touches can go wherever your imagination leads you. Simms's quilts include such flourishes as coins, lapel pins, and an actual fork with a shoelace "noodle" wrapped around it (a fun memory from a trip to Rome).

Simms's book explains the details on gathering supplies, transferring the images, and constructing your scrapbook quilt; and a dozen quilts are featured for inspiration. One was created in honor of Simms's mother's seventieth birthday and is adorned with more than 230 images. Another, entitled "Wedding Quilt," includes pressure-sensitive music boxes hidden inside patchwork pouches. One of the most touching quilts featured in Simms's book is called "Oh, My Papa!" and was created in honor of her father. The following story, taken from Simms's book, is a testament to how a quilt, particularly a scrapbook quilt, is more a labor of love than a craft.

"I made this quilt for my mother, but it's not entirely clear who has gotten the most out of it. My father died in 1984, and at the time this quilt was made my mother had been a widow for almost eight years. . . . She began to travel, and to teach, and to meet the challenges of life not as my father's wife, but as her own person. I saw her courage, and I watched her blossom under conditions she never would have chosen for herself. Looking back, I think she came to terms with his death sooner than I did. For a long time I was angry at my father for dying. I wish I had been been able to make this quilt sooner; I think it would have helped.

"Mother and I selected many of the pictures together from her stash of old photographs in the basement, from family photo albums, and from old cardboard boxes stored away long ago. As we sorted through the collection of photographs, deciding which ones to use, the oral history of our family was retold—the who's-who stories that one generation tells the next.

"One of the boxes we found in the basement hadn't been opened in over forty years! In it we found things of my father's dating back to World War II: newspaper clippings, documents, photographs, medals and insignia from his uniform, and a survival kit. The survival kit contained phrases in several foreign languages, a rusty six-inch sawblade in case he was captured, and a silk map of Europe, screened on both sides. A small strip of the map . . . is part of the quilt, as are his U.S. Army Air Force identification card, his Fort Collins library card, and the envelope which held the first letter he wrote to my mother from the convoy going overseas. I read the letter and saw a side of my father I had never seen before. I began to understand the powerful impact the war had on his life.

"The quilt also has photographs of Dad growing up. There's a picture of him on a bear rug, another of him throwing snowballs, still another posing by a trellis of roses. In the quilt he's a toddler in a Buster Brown haircut, a gangling teenager in a swimsuit, a new father with me in his arms, and the father-of-the-bride at my wedding. . . .

"Diplomas from the various universities my father attended are stitched up in this quilt, from his undergraduate degree to his Ph.D. So is the certificate he received from the Italian government when they made him a Knight of the Republic of Italy. The medal is there, too, and so is the green silk sash he was supposed to wear it on. Part of the silver I.D. bracelet my mother gave him when he went to war is stitched onto the quilt. So are his dog tags, and to me the most valuable item: the flat, well-worn metal thing that he carried on his key ring. I guess it was a screwdriver/bottle-opener combination. Whatever it was, I never remember him without it.

"The colors I picked for the quilt were the colors that reminded me of him—light browns, khaki greens, and mustard yellow. As I stitched this quilt I could feel him with me. With every picture I touched, I remembered. I could hear him laugh, I could see him walk, I could remember what it felt like as a child, to reach my arms around his middle and hug him, burying my face in his shirt.

"I laughed, I cried, I forgave."

THE EXPERIMENTAL AIRCRAFT ASSOCIATION'S
ANNUAL CONVENTION AND SPORT AIRCRAFT EXHIBITION

Oshkosh, Wisconsin

Michelle Prater Burke

Growing up with a father who was an air traffic controller, I was well-versed in the world of aviation. My father's seemingly built-in radar would quickly locate any plane overhead; he would educate me on the plane's model and his guess on its destination. Dad could recite the three-letter symbols for airports across the U.S. and tell fascinating stories about warplanes that saved the day with their aerial maneuvers. As a child, I considered becoming a pilot so that I too could guide a plane on some impossible mission. So I was not surprised to find myself visiting the Experimental Aircraft Association's Annual Convention and Sport Aircraft Exhibition in Oshkosh, Wisconsin. In Oshkosh, the impossible happens every year, and on a grand scale.

Last summer, as I neared Oshkosh, I could see a steady stream of planes descending over the Wisconsin landscape. Hundreds of thousands of people had already gathered to share a passion for aviation. I marveled at how this, the world's premier aviation event, had grown from such meager beginnings. The Experimental Aircraft Association (EAA) was founded in 1953 in the Milwaukee basement of Paul H. Poberezny. Soon after, Poberezny and a number of his friends who enjoyed building their own aircrafts organized the EAA's first fly-in convention at a nearby airfield. The event attracted only a few dozen people and a handful of homebuilt and antique aircraft.

Two years later, Poberezny published an article entitled "How to Build an Airplane for Less Than Eight Hundred Dollars." The article created tremendous interest and sent EAA memberships soaring. As the organization grew, so did the yearly fly-in. The event was moved several times to accommodate increasing numbers of people and airplanes. In 1970, the fly-in moved to its present home in Oshkosh. When I attended the event, I was among more than 850,000 people, many who had flown their planes from across the globe.

Pilots, designers, builders, families, and aviation enthusiasts of all ages gathered at the festival; a number came in search of information on building or restoring their own planes. These "amateur-built" or "custom-built" aircraft are licensed by the Federal Aviation Administration as "experimental." Working either from purchased kits or from plans, the builders spend anywhere from one thousand to three thousand hours to complete their projects, and some builders spend a decade or more on their creations.

Knowing the effort involved, I was amazed to realize how many on display were homebuilt. The amateur-built models were joined by a number of advanced-design aircraft and antique planes. Each had its own story. Sitting under the wing of a B-17, I listened as a silver-haired gentleman described flying over World War II Germany. I marveled as the owner of a kit-built speedster explained its ability to fly four hundred miles per hour; and I stood amazed as aerial performers showcased their talents.

At the end of my pilgrimage to Oshkosh, I was glad my father had shared his interest in aviation and that I had been a part of this celebration of flight. Evidently, thousands of modern-day Orville and Wilbur Wrights still believe in doing the impossible and flying through the clouds. Perhaps the American dream includes not only a white picket fence and your own piece of land, but a homebuilt plane in your own slice of the sky.

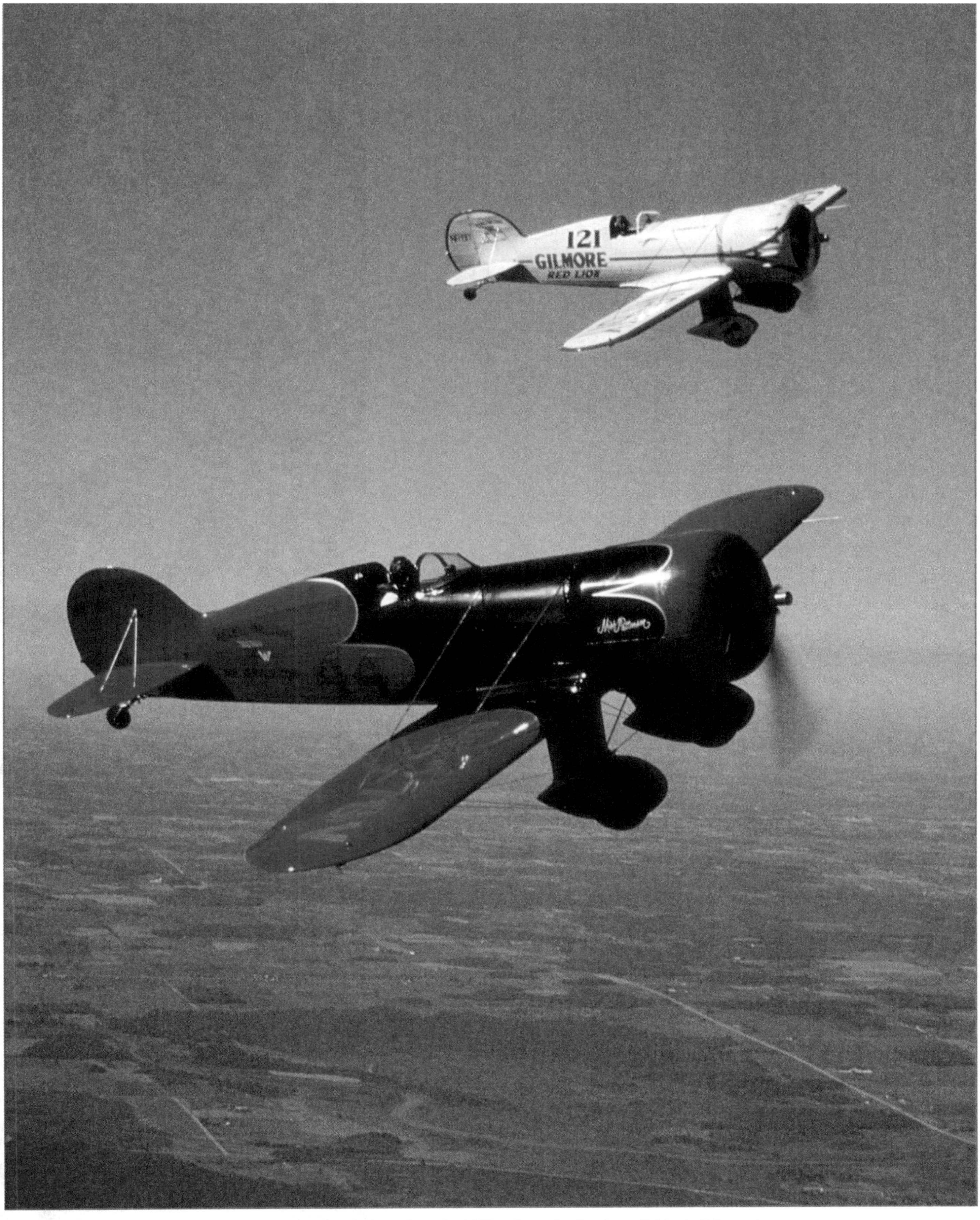
121
GILMORE
RED LION

Two restored racing airplanes from the 1930s take to the sky above Oshkosh, Wisconsin.

POSSESSION

Jane Merchant

I always owned the sky; the sky was mine
From the moment I first looked up at it, and felt
All the enormous tender brilliance shine
Into my wondering heart, where it has dwelt
Unceasingly. I own uncounted millions
Of stars, though using only two or three;
And as for clouds, of course, I've many trillions,
And the sun is my peculiar property.
My ownership of sky does not preclude
Others enjoying it; I'm glad to share
My glad possession of infinitude.
But any who come between us must beware
Since, whether lightning-lashed or rainbow-lit,
The sky belongs to me, and I to it.

HALF-
REMEMBERED
WINGS

Gail Brook Burket

There still are times man feels the need to soar
Above the stolid earth in pinioned flight,
To keep an eagle's rendezvous once more
Upborne on surging wings of ageless might,
To feel the lilting exultation known
By those who reach some ice-sculpted mountain spire
Whose pinnacle of never-trodden stone
Reflects the blazing sun's unclouded fire.

Encircled by blue boundaries of sky,
On baffling heights which plodding feet may climb,
We watch the earth-born clouds float lightly by
While thoughts glide swiftly through an eon's time—
Old memories of long forgotten things,
Untrammeled flight, and half-remembered wings.

A log balcony offers a spectacular view of Brookville, Ohio. Photo by Jessie Walker.

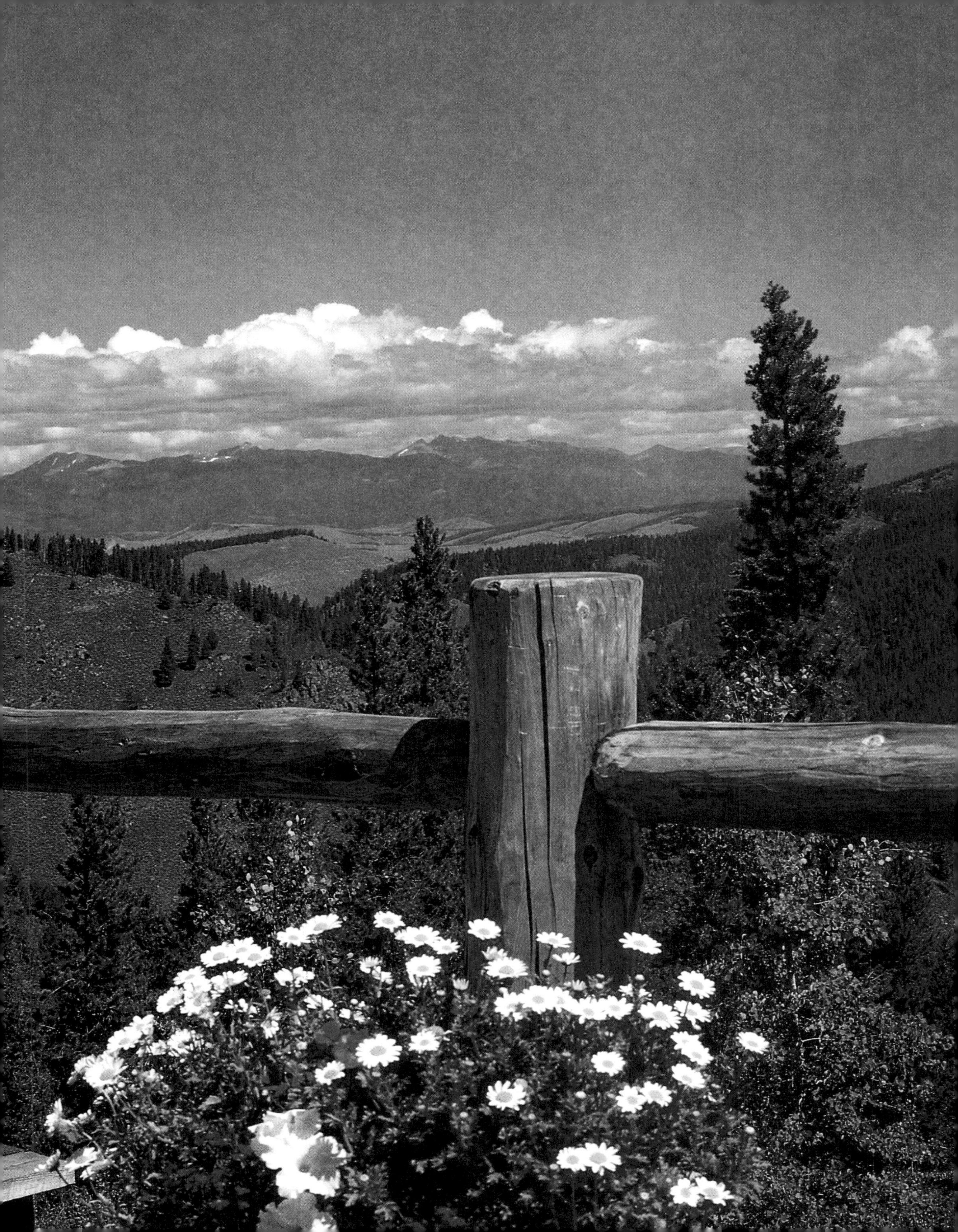

LEGENDARY AMERICANS

Christine M. Landry

AMELIA EARHART

When Amelia Earhart decided that she wanted to fly a plane, she asked her father to inquire about flying lessons; she feared that a woman would be ridiculed for her desire to fly. At the time, women in aviation were rare in America; but Earhart's luck, charm, and personality propelled her into aviation fame, and the attention she garnered ignited the acceptance of women pilots.

Born in 1897 in Atchison, Kansas, young Earhart was considered a tomboy who could "belly-flop" sleds just like the boys. She once designed a makeshift roller coaster, to the dismay of the adults; and she and her sister, Muriel, often played in the yard in their bloomers, horrifying the neighbors.

Earhart's father had difficulty keeping a job due to his alcoholism, and the family moved frequently. Amelia Earhart was forced to be self-sufficient at a young age; but by fellow classmates at her high school, she was viewed as a loner. She did not attend her high-school graduation ceremony, and the caption beneath her picture in her high-school yearbook read: "A. E.—the girl in brown who walks alone."

Earhart drifted following her graduation; she attended Ogontz College then dropped out to help with the war effort when World War I was declared. She worked as a nurse's aid, which eventually prompted her to enter Columbia University as a pre-medical student. The summer of 1920, she left school to be with her parents in Los Angeles.

Earhart and her father often went to air shows, which were popular during the 1920s. At one show, Earhart took her first ride in a plane. The experience so invigorated her that at dinner that evening she announced, "I think I'd like to fly." The offhanded remark would change her life.

Not long after her flying lessons began, Earhart decided "life was incomplete unless I owned a plane." She purchased a bi-plane, painted it yellow, and named it the *Canary*. Odd jobs helped her pay for the plane and the lessons and ranged from a clerk at a telephone company to hauling gravel in a truck.

On October 22, 1922, at the age of twenty-five, Earhart set her first flying record. She reached fourteen thousand feet—a new altitude record for women. When her engine faltered, she dove in a tailspin through the fog, pulling up only when she saw the ground. Seven months later, she became the sixteenth woman in the world to receive a pilot's license from the Fédération Aéronautique Internationale. In spite of these accomplishments, Earhart still considered flying only a hobby and never expected to make a career of it.

In 1924 Earhart sold her plane, bought a car, and moved to Boston to work as a social worker and teach English to immigrants. Her weekends were spent at a nearby airfield, flying. Once, in an introduction, she described herself as "a social worker who flies for sport." Soon, Amelia Earhart would become the most well-known woman aviator in the world.

In 1927 American aviation received a boost.

That year Charles Lindbergh's solo flight across the Atlantic Ocean made him a hero to the public, but a woman had yet to even cross the Atlantic as a passenger. Amy Phipps Guest, an American living in England, was sponsoring a transatlantic flight on which two men would serve as pilots. The third member of the crew was to be a woman. George Palmer Putnam, a promoter and publisher, was in charge of finding that woman, and Amelia Earhart was soon selected. Her pilot's license was considered a plus; and although she was not the pilot, she was named captain of the flight.

When a friend warned Earhart of the dangers in the transatlantic flight and urged her not to go, Earhart responded, "No, . . . my family's insured; there's only myself to think about. And when a great adventure's offered you—you don't refuse it, that's all."

The plane was named the *Friendship,* and it left Newfoundland on June 17, 1928, and landed in Wales. The flight took twenty hours and forty minutes and made Earhart the first woman to cross the Atlantic. The success of the flight propelled Earhart into the role of a celebrity, much to her surprise. As a passenger and not a pilot, she felt the attention was undeserved; but the public only found her modesty endearing, calling her "Lady Lindy" due to her physical resemblance to Charles Lindbergh.

George Putnam published a book by Earhart entitled *20 Hrs. 40 min.,* and the two were eventually married in 1931. Earhart discovered that Putnam not only encouraged her flying, he planned her publicity tours.

Longing to prove herself as a pilot worthy of the attention she had received, Earhart declared she would again cross the Atlantic, but this time, alone. At dusk on May 20, 1932, she left for the trip in her monoplane. From the beginning, the flight was plagued by problems. Her altimeter malfunctioned, leaving Earhart to guess at her altitude. When she encountered an electrical storm, she rose to avoid it, but at the higher altitude, her wings began to ice. Earhart was forced to lower the plane to an altitude where she was able to see the waves breaking in the ocean. She was so off course that she landed in a meadow located in Londonderry, Ireland. Thus Amelia Earhart was the first woman to complete a solo flight across the Atlantic, and she was greeted only by a herder and his cows.

At thirty-eight, Earhart said she had "just one more long flight in my system." She wanted that flight to be a trip around the world. Purdue University, where she was employed as a career counselor to women, gave her the vehicle in which she hoped to accomplish the task. Earhart called her well-equipped, twin-engine Lockheed Electra 10E her "flying laboratory." Her plan was to fly around the world at the Equator—the longest possible route for the journey and a feat never accomplished by a man or a woman.

On May 21, 1937, Amelia Earhart and her navigator, Fred Noonan, began their flight from Oakland, California, heading east. At their fuel stops, Earhart would send home pictures and articles about their experiences. The conditions she stayed in were often primitive, her flight schedule was grueling, and she suffered from fatigue. On June twenty-ninth, Earhart and Noonan landed in Lae, New Guinea. They had flown a total of 22,000 miles.

Their next destination was to be Howland Island, an island so small it would be difficult to visually locate, and after that, Hawaii and then home. The *Itasca,* a Coast Guard cutter, was to direct Earhart to the island by radio. During her flight to Howland Island, the Coast Guard's radio was unable to get enough clear contact from Earhart for them to get a bearing. At 8:44 A.M. they heard her say, "We are running north and south." It was the last they, or anyone else, heard from her. Amelia Earhart and Fred Noonan are presumed to have run out of gas, crashing into the Pacific Ocean.

A sixteen-day search uncovered no wreckage nor any sign of the crew. The mystery surrounding the disappearance turned Amelia Earhart from a celebrity to a legend. Speculation on the cause of her death or possible survival continues today. Earhart once said, "When I go, I would like to go in my plane. Quickly." Most likely, she did.

The attention Amelia Earhart brought to women in aviation has had lasting positive effects. In a letter to her husband about the around-the-world flight, Earhart wrote of the ambition women must have: "Please know I am quite aware of the hazards. I want to do it because I want to do it. Women must try to do things as men have tried. When they fail, failure must be but a challenge to others."

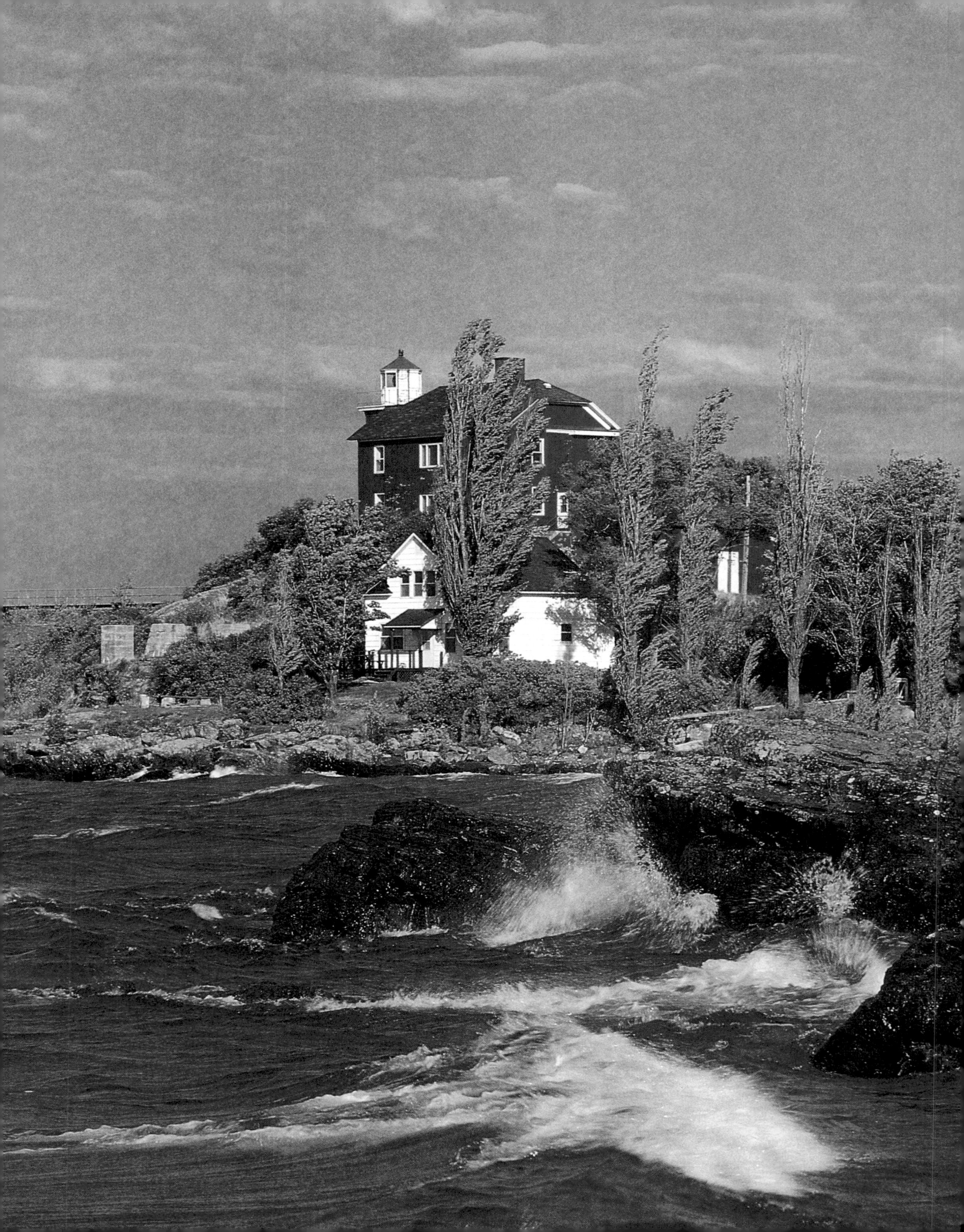

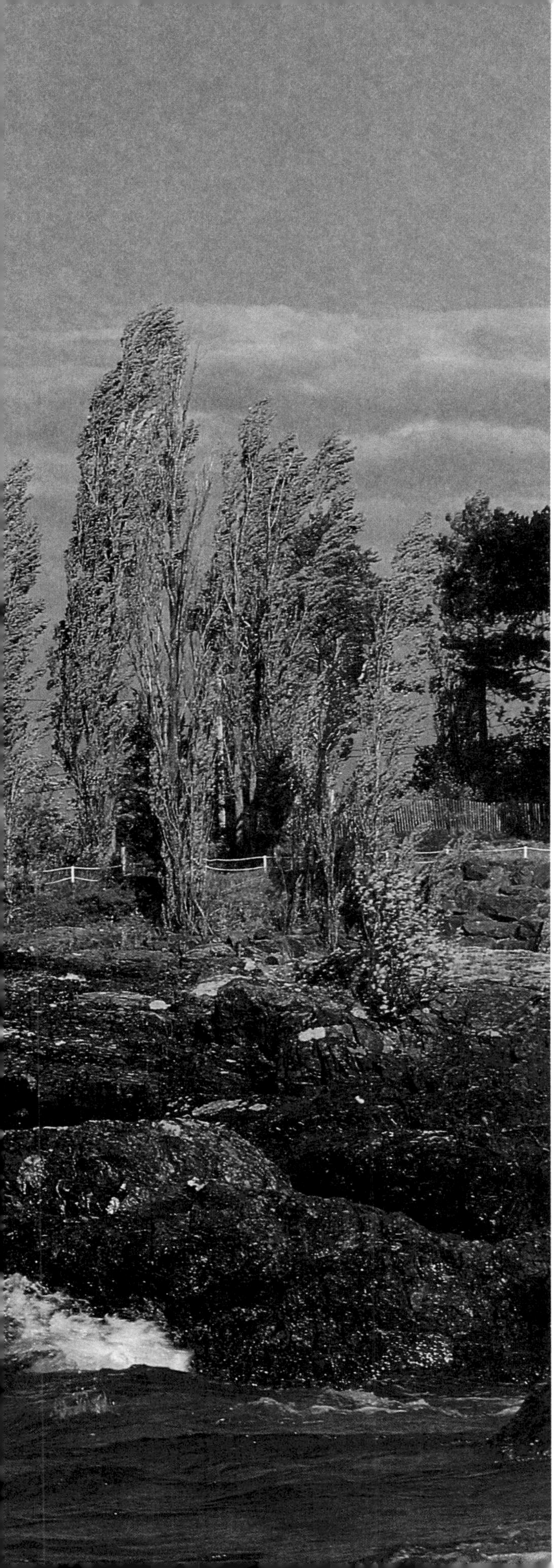

Someday, Sometime

Agnes Davenport Bond

Someday, sometime,
I like to think I shall go back
To all the places I have loved.
To travel on the sea again,
To bathe again in flying surf,
And lie again on warm beach sands
On some far island shore.
To climb the mountain sides,
To camp far back in virgin woods,
And sit around a blazing fire at night,
With moonlight hanging in the pines.
To sleep again on sweet pine boughs,
To hear throughout the peaceful night
The music of a stream close by,
Or of a distant waterfall.
Someday, sometime, I shall go back
Because a little part of me
Is left behind in places I have loved,
And so I like to think I shall go back,
Someday, sometime.

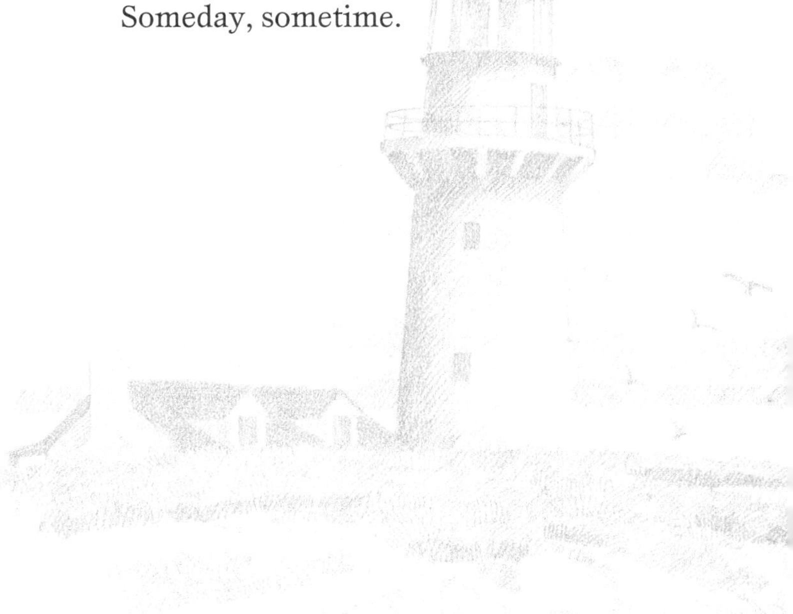

In Marquette, Michigan, Marquette Lighthouse stands watch over Lake Superior. Photo by Darryl R. Beers.

COLLECTOR'S CORNER

Matthew R. Brown

As a young child, I was an avid reader and spent many an hour dreaming of the far-off lands and adventures described in my books. My family smiled patiently as I insisted that I would become a world traveler when I grew up. I would find a flying carpet in India and discover a den of lions in Africa. No destination seemed unreachable to my youthful mind. But at the age of fourteen, an auto accident left me confined to a wheelchair, and I felt like my dreams of adventure had ended. How could I travel freely if I were unable to walk? On my next birthday, a beloved aunt, who was a seasoned traveler herself, gave me an inexpensive present that changed my outlook and my future.

Found in an antique store, the gift was a slightly faded, illustrated map of India during the days of British imperialism. On the back my aunt had written, "Matthew, your flying carpet is waiting; I have no doubt you will find it." The thoughtful gift renewed my spirit and gave me hope that my dream of traveling could still come true, even in a wheelchair.

Over the next several years, I continued to receive maps from friends and relatives who hoped to encourage me to follow my dreams. Each map was a sort of geographical snapshot of the world, slowly revealing how the earth was discovered and plotted. One from my older brother charted our hometown (and favorite fishing hole) almost one hundred years ago. From a childhood friend I received a map that pictured Virginia, my birth state, when its borders were first formed. But my favorite maps were always of the lands I hoped to visit in the future.

I began learning more about my collection by attending lectures at a nearby museum, and I even became the youngest member of a local map society. With my newfound knowledge, I searched for the history behind each map I owned. As I studied them, the stories of pirates and adventurers I had read as a child came back to me; and I found myself wondering if a map of the Caribbean had once been used to search for sunken treasure or if an explorer had read another map by moonlight as he navigated through the Rockies.

After I graduated from college, I sat down with the old army trunk where I stored my maps and began planning my first adventure. As I sorted through my small collection, I considered a train ride down the west coast of California or a simple car trip to see old family friends in Canada. But as I considered my options, I soon realized there was no real question where my first destination would be—India, in honor of the first map I'd received from my aunt, the map that reassured me that the world could still be mine.

I now travel fairly regularly, sometimes a great distance but more often within my region to large antique auctions or exhibitions, where I hope to find interesting additions to my growing collection of maps. One of my favorites was found in a dusty folder at a West Coast print shop. Inside was an early twentieth-century map rendering the region of California where my grandfather (and namesake) had traveled to seek his fortune in 1910. The most valuable piece in my collection is a seventeenth-century map of the world that was created by a well-known cartographer, or mapmaker, of the time. It hangs on my bedroom wall as a constant reminder of all the places I have yet to see.

Although my vacations can be challenging and must be planned carefully, my travels are limited mainly by my checkbook and my company's vacation policy, the same difficulties that plague all travel buffs, handicapped or not. Thanks to a long-ago gift from a wise aunt, I have been able to see my childhood dreams become reality. Each new map I add to my collection holds the promise of another place to explore, and another flying carpet that awaits.

THE RIGHT DIRECTION

If you would like to collect maps, the following information will be helpful:

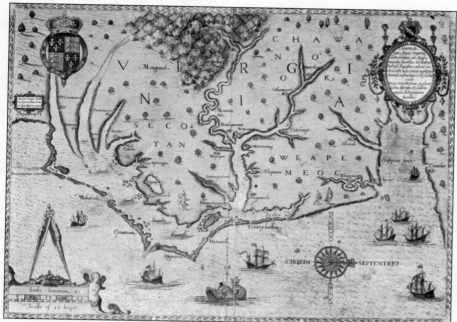

This map of Virginia was created by Netherlandish cartographer Theodor de Bry (1528–1598). Image from Superstock.

HISTORY

• Maps were once highly sought-after instruments of power that gave monarchs the key to private trade routes and newly discovered lands.

• One of the earliest wall maps, now five hundred years old, was created by a German scholar and measures four by eight feet. The world map reflects much guesswork—Cuba is as large as Great Britain.

• Maps were prized for their beauty as early as the late sixteenth century, when alchemist John Dee noted, "Some, to beautify their halls, parlors, chambers . . . liketh, loveth, getteth and useth maps, charts and geographical globes."

• In Holland, the seventeenth century is known as the "golden age of cartography." During this time period, the Dutch (who are known as master mariners) made map making an art.

• One of the most important maps in the history of America is the Mitchell Map, which was used to negotiate the Treaty of Paris in 1783. Today it is worth approximately $60,000.

• Many universities, libraries, and museums display map collections that can teach the new collector. Local map societies offer lectures and information for map enthusiasts.

INTERESTING FINDS

• Maps that feature elaborate border designs (often picturing sea monsters or perilous seas) and that were usually created for the upper class.

• Early maps of the New World that differ dramatically from its actual appearance.

• Maps in different languages.

• Antique maps featuring the region or country where one's ancestors originated.

• Maps picturing one's hometown or favorite vacation spot in early eras.

• Battle maps that chart military history.

PURCHASE AND CARE

• Serious collectors recommend first buying for enjoyment instead of investment purposes.

• Centuries-old maps that are not in perfect condition are sold for as little as fifteen dollars. Decorative maps from as early as the 1600s can be found for a small investment of $100 to $200.

• Saltwater stains, age-cracks, foxing, and period overwriting, although adding character, can lower a map's value.

• Beware of purchasing antique maps that are already framed. The frame may hide tattered edges, brittle paper, or a modern print date.

• When framing an old map, use only archival quality glass and papers and water-soluble adhesives. Also, never allow the glass to rest directly on the map.

• Store or hang maps away from damaging sunlight, heat, and humidity.

BITS & PIECES

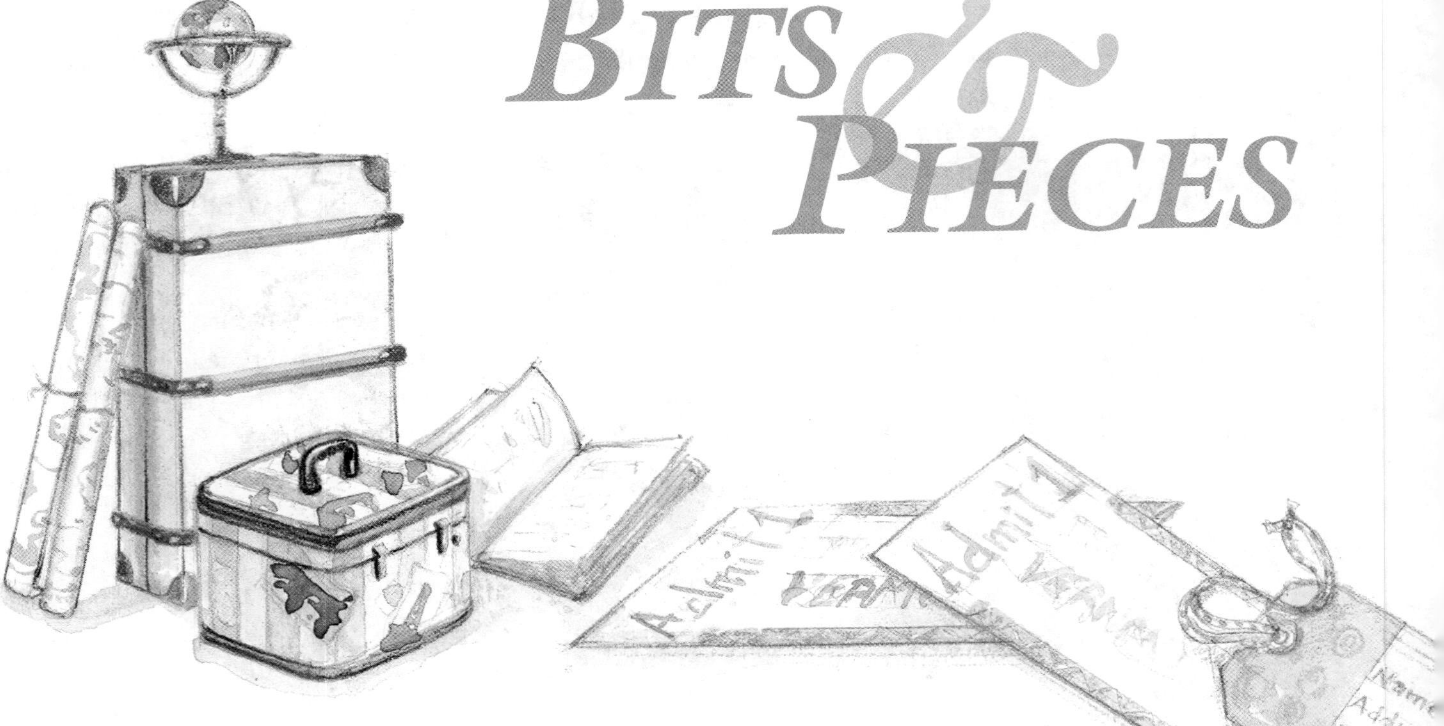
Admit 1
Admit 1
Name
Address
Phone

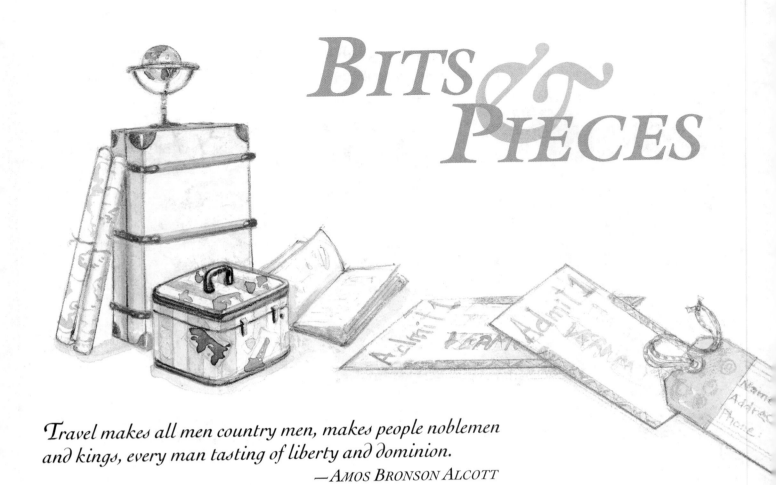

Travel makes all men country men, makes people noblemen and kings, every man tasting of liberty and dominion.

—AMOS BRONSON ALCOTT

You travel wide and far to scout and see and search;
If God you fail to see, you have nothing observed.

—ANGELUS SILESIUS

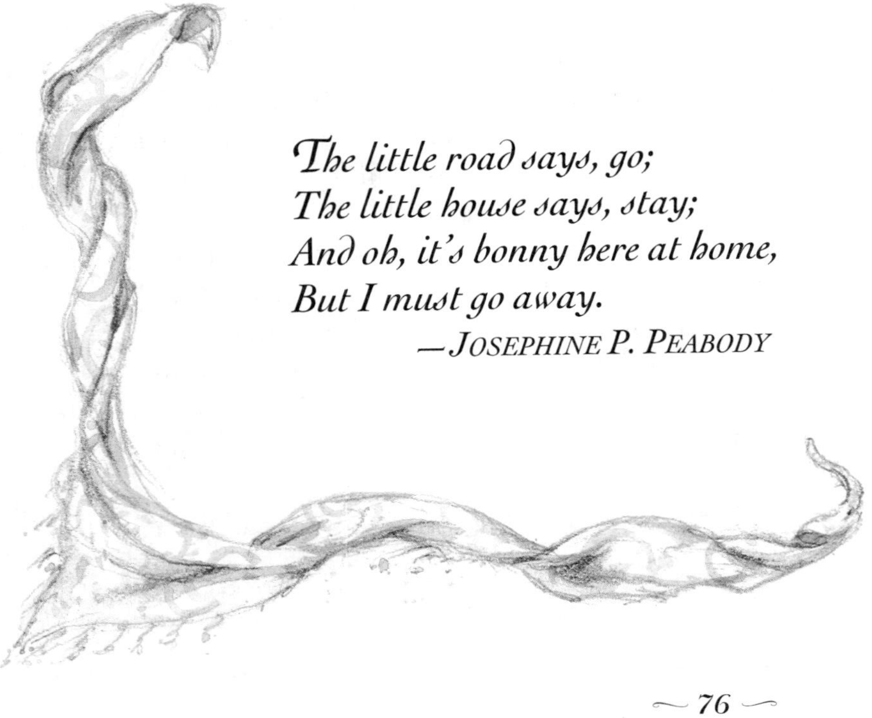

The little road says, go;
The little house says, stay;
And oh, it's bonny here at home,
But I must go away.

—JOSEPHINE P. PEABODY

Good company in a journey makes the way to seem the shorter.

—IZAAK WALTON

Life is like a journey, taken on a train,
with a pair of travelers at each window pane.
I may sit beside you all the journey through;
or I may sit elsewhere, never knowing you.
But if fate should mark me to sit at your side,
let's be pleasant travelers — it's so short a ride.
—AUTHOR UNKNOWN

Go far, too far you cannot, still the
farther the more experience finds you.
—FRANCIS BEAUMONT

In traveling I shape myself betimes
to idleness and take fools' pleasure.
—GEORGE ELIOT

A wise traveler never despises
his own country.
—GOLDONI

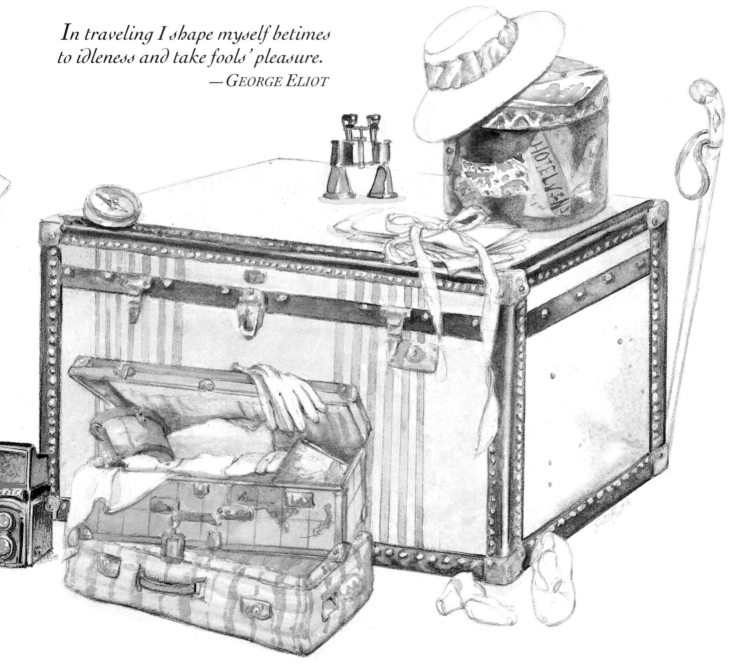

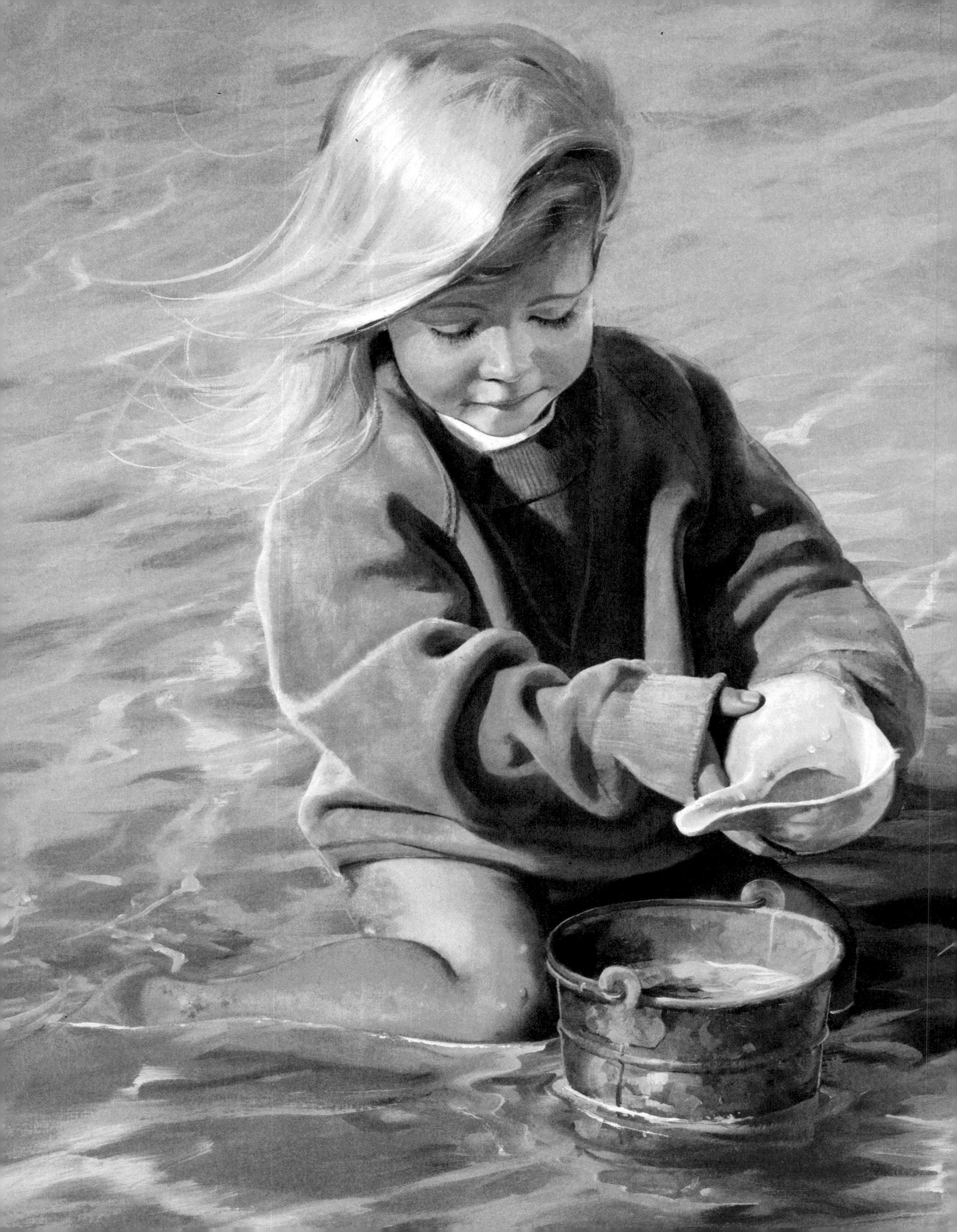

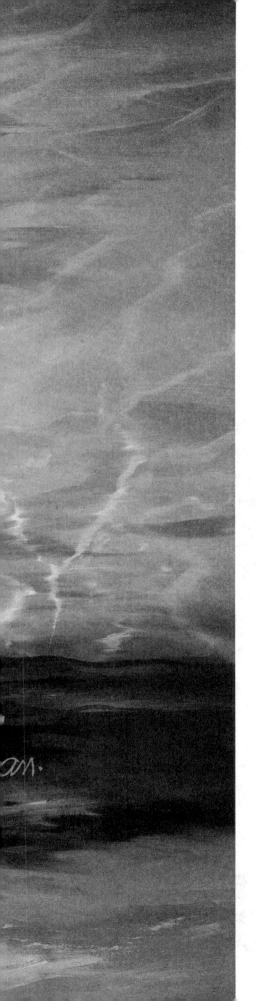

FOR THE CHILDREN

THE ISLAND

A. A. Milne

If I had a ship,
I'd sail my ship,
I'd sail my ship
Through Eastern seas;
Down to a beach where the slow waves thunder—
The green curls over and the white falls under—
Boom! Boom! Boom!
On the sun-bright sand.
Then I'd leave my ship and I'd land,
And climb the steep white sand.

And climb to the trees,
The six dark trees,
The coconut trees on the cliff's green crown—
Hands and knees
To the coconut trees,
Face to the cliff as the stones patter down,
Up, up, up,
staggering, stumbling,
Round the corner where the rock is crumbling,
Round this shoulder,
Over this boulder,
Up to the top where the six trees stand. . . .

And there would I rest, and lie,
My chin in my hands, and gaze
At the dazzle of sand below,
And the green waves curling slow,
And the grey-blue distant haze
Where the sea goes up to the sky. . . .
And I'd say to myself as I looked so
lazily down at the sea:
"There's nobody else in the world,
and the world was made for me."

A girl discovers the sea in Donald Zolan's painting SUMMER'S CHILD.

Water in the House

S. Omar Barker

She comes no more to fill her pail
In the cool, dark spring. The winding trail
Grows grassy, and halfway across
Her kneeling stone, green velvet moss
Already creeps in timid token
Of abandonment. The broken
Remnants of an old stone jar
Lie listless where the lace ferns are.

The singing woman comes no more.
Carrying water is a chore
Less burdensome for pipes — and yet
Can any spring so soon forget
A woman's swinging water pail
Flashing brightly down the trail,
Or the deep familiar pull
As she knelt to dip it full?

A spring offers its water in PROVENCAL SPRING, 1903 *by Henry Herbert La Thangue (1859–1929). Bradford City Art Galleries and Museums, West Yorkshire, UK/Bridgeman Art Library, London/New York/Superstock.*

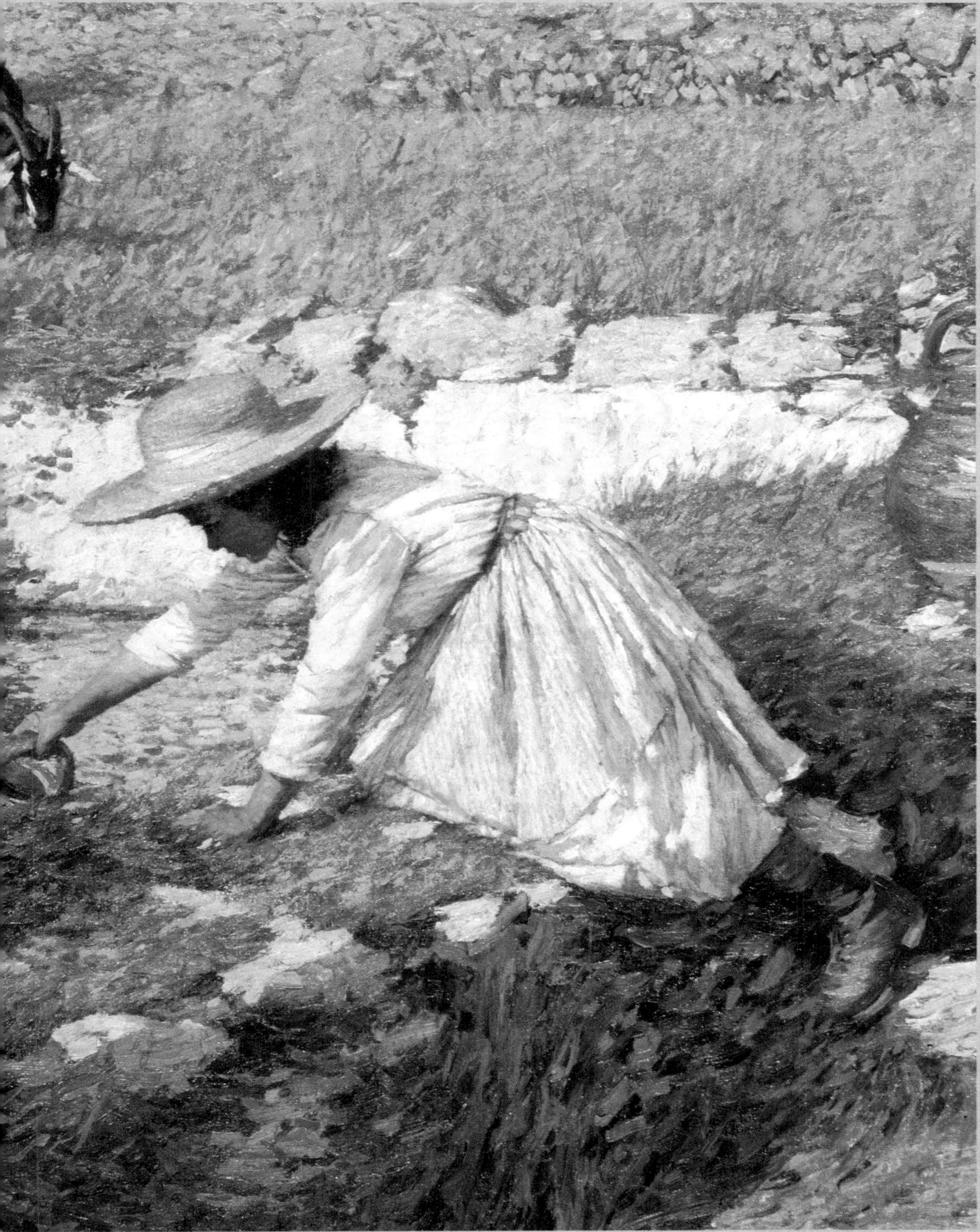

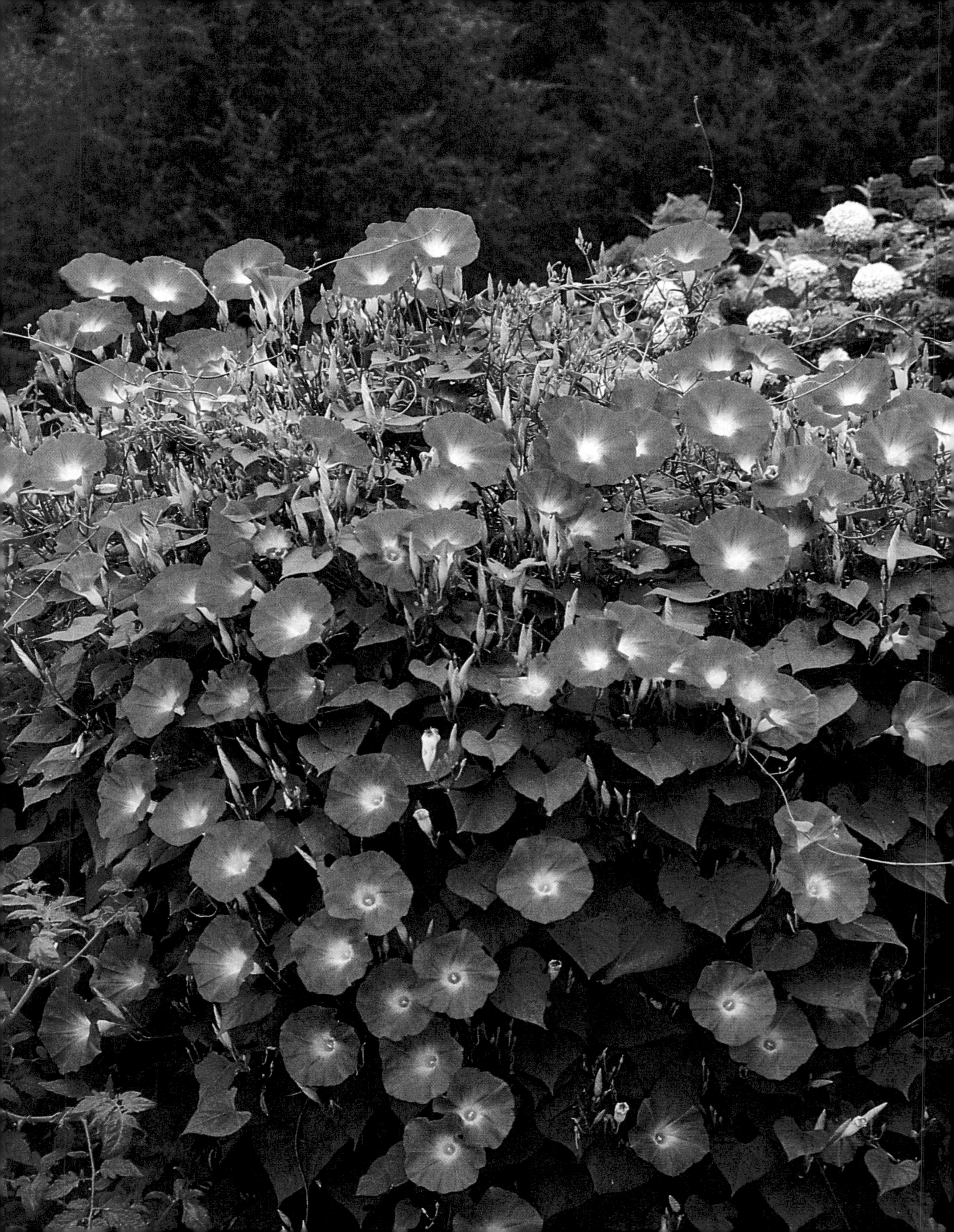

Trumpets of Dawn

D. A. Hoover

Cradled in the lap of summer,
Morning glory blossoms shine
Bright with dawn's first crystal dewdrops,
Tender trumpets of the vine.
Color-feast of August rainbow—
Purple, blue, magenta, white—
Living, fairy-tinted canvas
Unveiled from the robe of night.

Morning Glory

Becky Jennings

There's a blue cloud on my trellis
Every morning, born anew;
Lovely flowering morning glories
Sparkling bright with drops of dew.

In the noon sun they will fade away
Like a haunting sweet refrain,
But I know with each new sunrise,
The blue cloud will come again.

Morning glories drape a trellis in Missouri. Photo by Gay Bumgarner.

Summer in a Pail

Mamie Ozburn Odum

My garden blooms in silence dim and cool,
And each brown seed sleeps snugly in its place
As Johnny-jump-ups dance around the pool
Where fish float by with golden fins of lace.
I till the soil, and I am resolute
That beauty on this fertile spot must grow;
Apple-cheeked clouds
cradle each tiny shoot
That truants from
its regal mother-row.

Flowers, from flower-land
of every hue,
flutter and socialize
in golden sun,
Stand cool and fragrant
in the falling dew;
Flowers to please the heart
of every one.
My garden waits,
colorful and frail,
That I may bring home
summer in a pail.

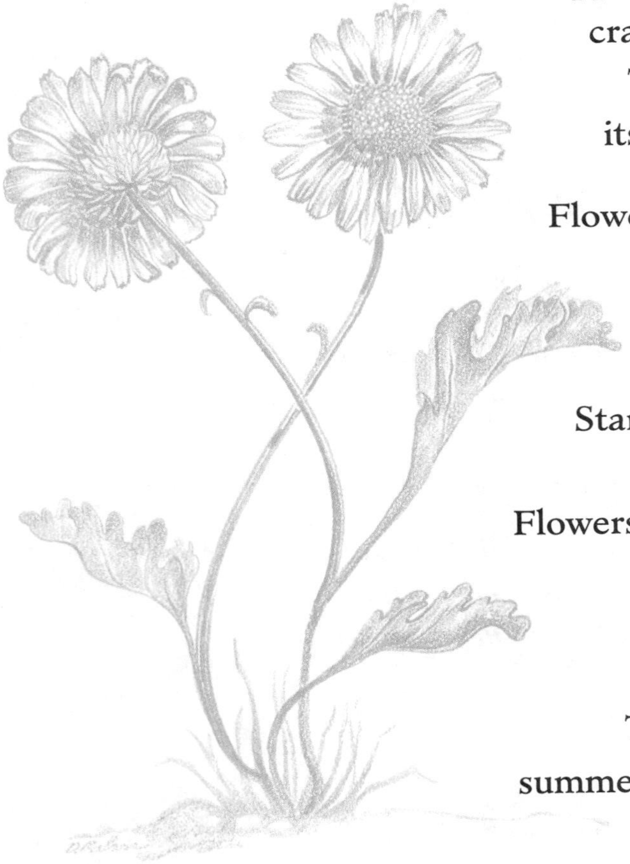

A well-used watering can is dressed with a bounty of blooms. Photo by Nancy Matthews.

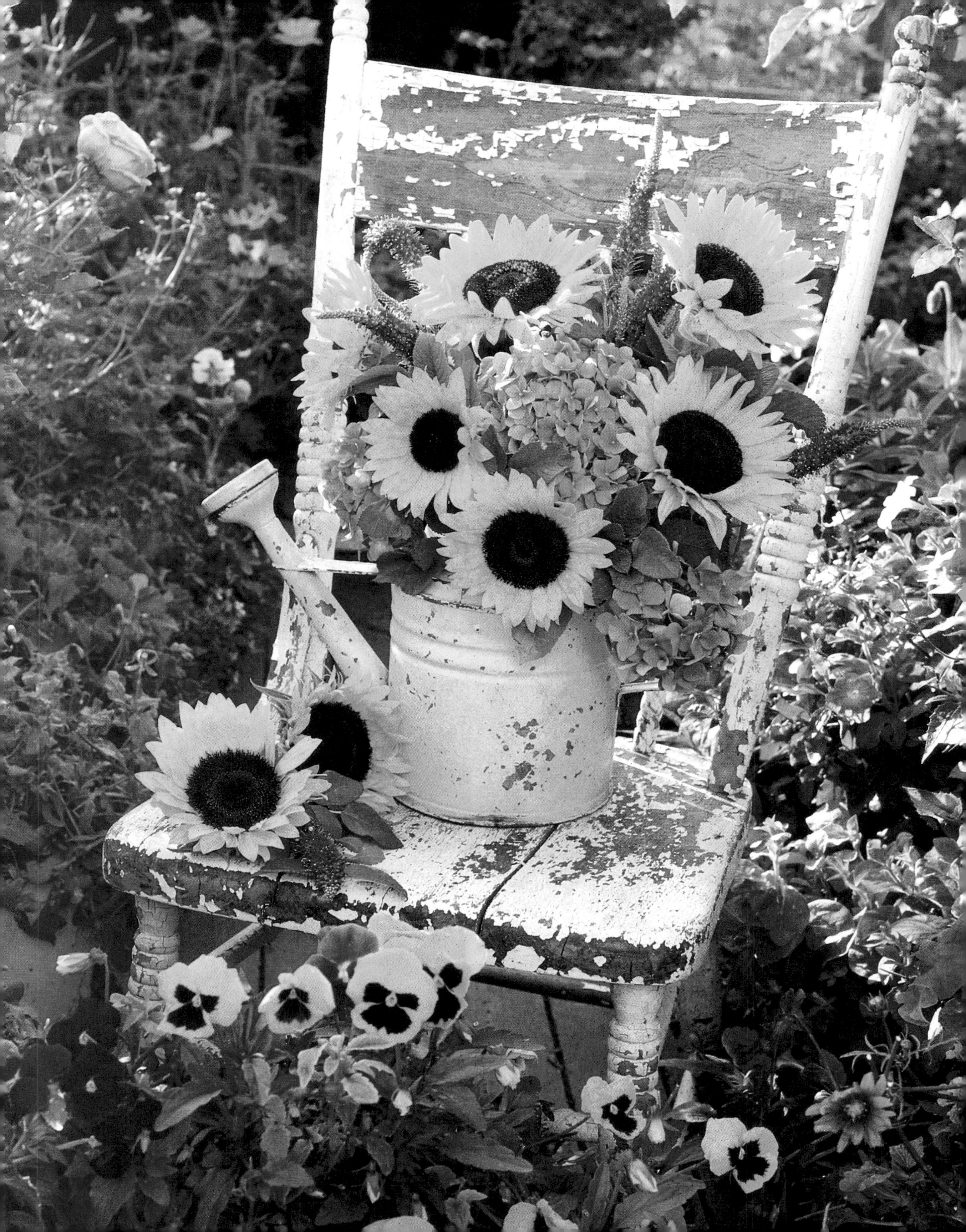

★ ★ ★ Readers' Forum ★ ★ ★

Snapshots from Our Ideals Readers

Above: Diane Riddell is proud to share this photo of her grandchildren, R. J. and Hayden Boudreau, ages six and three. The children took part in the Fourth of July celebration in Diane's hometown of Irvine, California. Each year, the children in the community decorate their bicycles and wagons (or even their pets!) and parade down the street to show their patriotism.

Left: Four-year-old Max Michael O'Brien sees visions of strawberry jam as he sits among the fruit in his grandfather's berry patch. The photo was sent to us by Max Michael's grandparents, Joyce and Roger L. Garrison of Rochester, New York.

Far right: Connie Smith of Canton, Georgia, tells us that although her house is formal, she fills her backyard with such rustic favorites as this wagon wheel. Keeping two tiny hands on the wheel is Connie's granddaughter Victoria Ansley Wymer.

Above: Mrs. Leland Wentzell of Nova Scotia, Canada, says her twenty-one-month-old grandson, Linden Corkum, adores taking nature walks and picking fistfuls of blooms for his mommy. In this snapshot, Linden is considering adding a daisy to his next bouquet.

Thank you Diane Riddell, Joyce and Roger Garrison, Connie Smith, and Mrs. Leland Wentzell for sharing your family photographs with *Ideals*. We hope to hear from other readers who would like to share snapshots with the *Ideals* family. Please include a self-addressed, stamped envelope if you would like the photos returned. Keep your original photographs for safekeeping and send duplicate photos along with your name, address, and telephone number to:

Readers' Forum
Ideals Publications Inc.
P.O. Box 305300
Nashville, Tennessee 37230

ideals

Publisher, Patricia A. Pingry
Editor, Michelle Prater Burke
Prepress Manager, Eve DeGrie
Designer, Peggy Murphy-Jones
Copy Editor, Kristi Richardson
Editorial Assistant, Christine M. Landry
Contributing Editors, Lansing Christman, Deana Deck, Pamela Kennedy

ACKNOWLEDGMENTS

BENNETT, GERTRUDE RYDER. "Pear Tree" from *The Harvesters* by Gertrude Ryder Bennett, 1967. Reprinted by permission of Golden Quill Press. BURKET, GAIL BROOK. "Half-Remembered Wings." Reprinted by permission of Anne E. Burket. COFFIN, ROBERT P. TRISTRAM. "The Secret Heart" from *Poems for a Son with Wings* by Robert P. Tristram Coffin. Copyright © 1945 by The Macmillan Company. Copyright renewal © 1972 by Richard N. Coffin, Margaret Coffin Halvosa, Mary Alice Westcott, and Robert P. T. Coffin, Jr. Reprinted by permission of Scribner, an imprint of Simon & Schuster, Inc. JAQUES, EDNA. "The Picnic to the Hills" from *Uphill All the Way*. Published in Canada by Thomas Allen & Son Limited. MILNE, A. A. "The Island" from *When We Were Very Young* by A. A. Milne. Copyright © 1924, E. P. Dutton & Co., Inc. Copyright renewed © 1952, A. A. Milne. Reprinted by arrangement with Dutton Children's Books, a division of Penguin Putnam, Inc. MURTON, JESSIE WILMORE. "And Never Knew" from *The Shining Thread*. Printed by courtesy of Pacific Press Publishing Association, Inc., Nampa ID. ROETHKE, THEODORE. "The Rose," copyright © 1963 by Beatrice Roethke, Administratrix of the Estate of Theodore Roethke. From *The Collected Poems of Theodore Roethke*. Used by permission of Doubleday, a division of Random House, Inc. SIMMS, AMI. Selection from *Creating Scrapbook Quilts*. Used by permission of Mallery Press. To contact Ami Simms, write Mallery Press at 4206 Sheraton Drive, Flint, Michigan 48532. Our sincere thanks to the following authors whom we were unable to locate: Sylvia Trent Auxier for "To Illustrate," Agnes Davenport Bond for "Someday, Sometime," Arthur Fischer for "For Loveliness," Jane Merchant for "Scent of Childhood" and "Possessions," Della Crowder Miller for "Summer Walks Again," and Martha D. Tourison for "Heritage."

My Heart's Request

Remelda Nielsen Gibson

Pink roses scent the gentle summer breeze;
Red-breasted robins hop upon the lawn.
White clouds contrast with alder-green of trees;
Verbena-blue commands the sky at dawn.

Star-yellow stalk charms butterfly and bee;
Gay hummingbird is trumpet flower's guest.
Petunias in my garden help me see
A hundred reasons for my heart's request:

Let summer stay a little longer, Time.
Let all minds photograph this pantomime.

Summer Serenade

Nora M. Bozeman

Flowers in profusion lie
On every sun-scorched hill.
I hear an August lullaby
From a lazy whippoorwill.
Softly, breezes kiss my cheek
And in my heart instill
A longing for sweet summertime
That she alone fulfills.